Aleksandr
Pushkin

Aleksandr Pushkin

Poet for the People

J.R. CHANEY

Lerner Publications Company • Minneapolis

Library of Congress Cataloging-in-Publication Data

Chaney, J.R.
    Aleksandr Pushkin : poet for the people / by J.R. Chaney.
        p.   cm.
    Includes bibliographical references and index.
    Summary: A biography of the first Russian writer to write in the
Russian language, a poet who was often called the "Father of Russian
Literature."
    ISBN 0-8225-4911-5 (lib. bdg.)
    1. Pushkin, Aleksandr Sergeevich, 1799-1837 — Biography — Juvenile
literature. 2. Poets, Russian — 19th century — Biography — Juvenile
literature. [1. Pushkin, Aleksandr Sergeevich, 1799-1837.
2. Poets, Russian.] I. Title.
PG3350.C46   1991
891.71'3 — dc20
[B]   91-14669
                                                                              CIP
                                                                               AC

Manufactured in the United States of America

Contents

Map appears on page 6

Russia in the Early 1800s

FINLAND

Miles
0   100   200   300   400

0   200   400   600
Kilometers

Baltic Sea

Neva River

Tsarskoye Selo

St. Petersburg

SIBERIA

Pskov

Mikhailovskoye

Malinniki

Volga River

Moscow

Moskva River

Boldino

Dneper River

Orenburg

Kiev

Yekaterinoslav

Kishinev

Odessa

CRIMEA

Gurzuf

Bakhchisaray

CAUCASUS

CAUCASUS MOUNTAINS

Caspian Sea

Black Sea

Tiflis

GEORGIA

OTTOMAN EMPIRE

Erzurum

TURKEY

Note to the Reader

Each Russian child is given three names. The first name is a given name, such as Aleksandr. The second name is a patronymic: the child's father's first name with a suffix— either "evna" or "ovna" for girls, and "evich" or "ovich" for boys. For example, Sergey Lvovich Pushkin named his son Aleksandr Sergeyevich Pushkin. And Aleksandr Sergeyevich Pushkin named his daughter Maria Aleksandrovna Pushkin. The last name is the family name, such as Pushkin.

Aleksandr Sergeyevich Pushkin, great-grandson of an African slave, was a thoughtful, silent child who would someday write about the world he observed around him.

⋗ ONE ⋖

The Quiet Dreamer
1799-1811

In the old Russian city of St. Petersburg, Arina
Rodionovna was taking a walk in a large park. In her arms
she held a baby, bundled up warmly against the cold wind.
She wandered beneath the trees beside the quiet road.
Suddenly she heard the sound of horses. A shiny carriage
approached, led by soldiers in bright coats and dark furry
hats. The people all stood still. They took off their hats
and bowed. Even the children held their furry caps in their
hands and waited until the carriage passed before going
back to play.

Arina also bowed her head to the carriage. As she did,
she heard a voice inside the carriage order the driver to stop.
It was the voice of the Russian tsar, or emperor, Paul I.
Everyone knew how dangerous it was to anger Paul. People
would say that the farther they were from Paul, the better.
The tsar was afraid the Russian people would rebel against
him the way the French had rebelled against King Louis XVI

in 1789. Paul I outlawed all modern clothing of the kind worn in France. He ordered the people to take off their hats and bow in his presence.

From high in his carriage, Tsar Paul scowled at the baby in Arina's arms. He shouted at Arina, ordering her to remove the child's headgear. The startled nanny had forgotten that the baby was wearing its bonnet. Still bowing, she quickly untied it and pulled it off.

The busy seaport of St. Petersburg—now Leningrad—at the end of the 18th century

When the carriage had passed, Arina rushed home, shaking with fear. The child she carried was Aleksandr Sergeyevich Pushkin. The nanny told Aleksandr's parents about the terrible event. They too were afraid — so afraid that they soon left St. Petersburg and returned to the city of Moscow to get farther away from Paul I. Aleksandr later wrote, "I have seen three emperors in my life. The first, Paul, ordered me to take off my hat and, since I was too young to be scolded, he scolded my nurse instead." This early confrontation seemed to be a sign of future trouble.

Russia's greatest poet was born in Moscow on June 6, 1799. He was the eldest son of Sergey Lvovich Pushkin and Nadezhda Osipovna Pushkin. Aleksandr was a fat child, with a soft, round face. His lips were thick and his dark hair grew in tight curls. He had remarkably bright, dreamy eyes. Until he was seven or eight years old, he hardly ever laughed. He was silent and not interested in his toys. He stayed close to his nurse, Arina. One of Aleksandr's earliest memories was of the Moscow earthquake on October 14, 1802. It rocked the house, making the lamps, tables, and chairs dance about. Many people couldn't believe their eyes and thought they were having a dizzy spell.

Aleksandr grew up in old Moscow. At the center of the city beside the Moskva River stood the Kremlin, Moscow's red-walled fortress. In Aleksandr's time, the tsar ruled the country from his palace in the northern city of St. Petersburg. Moscow was less important. However, even at that time it was the home of many small government offices. Aleksandr's father, Sergey, was a minor official of the government.

The Pushkin family came from old Russian nobility; many of them had been high officials and others had been rebels. Aleksandr was proud of his noble heritage and of his African ancestry. On his mother's side, Aleksandr was the great-grandson of Abram Hannibal, who was brought to Russia as a slave from northeastern Africa around 1700. Peter the Great—tsar from 1682 to 1725—adopted Hannibal into his care and gave him a French education. Hannibal eventually became the engineer-general of Russia.

Aleksandr's father was a member of the old Russian nobility. The nobility were those families who were specially honored by the tsar and owned large areas of land. By Aleksandr's time, the old nobility no longer fought battles for the tsars. Instead, they had the role of improving Russian culture.

The tsars before and after Paul I wanted Russia to be more like the European nations, especially France. French was spoken at the tsar's court in St. Petersburg. The upper classes spoke and wrote French. They paid for French plays to be performed in their homes. Aleksandr himself grew up reading the great French classics he found on the shelves of his father's library.

Although Aleksandr often was penniless as an adult, his family had once been quite wealthy. They became poorer and poorer because Sergey and Nadezhda did not know how to manage their money or their property. The Pushkins had trouble paying their rent. Their horses were bony and their carriages old. Some of their rooms were beautifully decorated with the finest antique furniture, while others remained bare and shabby. Nadezhda bought many fine gowns, but she had to borrow plates and wine glasses from her neighbors.

Sergey and Nadezhda had four children: Olga Sergeyevna, born in 1797; Aleksandr Sergeyevich, born in 1799; Nikolay

Sergey Lvovich Pushkin, below, *was Aleksandr's aloof father. Nadezhda Osipovna Pushkin,* below right, *disliked her son Aleksandr, who resembled her African grandfather, Abram Hannibal,* right.

Aleksandr at two years old

Sergeyevich, born in 1801; and Lev Sergeyevich, born in 1805. The children were generally ignored by their parents and were given over first to the nursemaids and later to a tutor — a teacher who lived in the house and taught them French and mathematics. One tutor replaced another. Some were fired, and some quit because they were not always paid on time. Aleksandr hated most of them. One tutor spent most of his time playing cards with the servants until he was caught and thrown out. Another made fun of Aleksandr's first poems.

Sergey Lvovich Pushkin was like many other fathers of the 19th century. He wanted to know that the children were healthy, but otherwise, he did not wish to see them. Nadezhda Osipovna Pushkin's favorite was her daughter Olga. But she disliked her eldest son because he resembled her African grandfather and her father, whom she despised. When she was annoyed, she would not hesitate to slap Aleksandr in front of the family. At his dance lessons, she once grew so impatient with his clumsiness that she took him by the ear and threw him out of the room, calling him "Monster!" Olga later wrote that Aleksandr was clumsy simply because he was so fat. But he was also made awkward by the fear and hurt he always felt under his mother's cold gaze.

With a bitter mother and a distant father, Aleksandr felt alone and unwanted in his own home. Fortunately, in a house almost swarming with serfs — servants who were owned as slaves — there were always other people to give him attention. His visits to the servants' rooms amused him when he was bored or lonely. He was loved and comforted as well by his nanny, Arina, and by his grandmother, Maria Alekseyevna Hannibal, who took a special liking to her chubby, curly-haired grandson.

He was most comfortable of all with his nanny. She was a great talker, and he an eager listener. Aleksandr loved to sit beside her as she knitted and listen to her chat about local deaths, marriages, and affairs; about the neighbor who had lost money gambling or the man who had recently beaten his wife.

Because his parents and their guests always spoke French, Aleksandr learned Russian only from his grandmother and Arina. His grandmother spoke and wrote perfect Russian. He would often run to her when he fled from his French tutors. As a young boy, he liked to sit in her sewing basket while she worked. She told exciting stories. In a poem Aleksandr wrote in flowing Russian in 1816, he recalls the strong effect that his grandmother had on his young imagination:

I love the memories of my childhood years.
O, how can I keep silent about my granny,
About the wonders of the mysterious nights,
When wearing a cap and her old-fashioned dress,
Having frightened away the evil spirits with a prayer,
She would make the sign of the cross over me devoutly
And begin telling me in a whisper
Of dead men, of Bova's exploits . . .
Terrified, I did not dare to stir,
Holding my breath, I would curl up under the blankets
Not feeling my arms or my head.
A single candle in a clay candlestick under the ikon
Dimly lit up the deep wrinkles,
The precious antique, my grandmother's cap
And her wide mouth, in which two teeth chattered.
Everything aroused a helpless panic in my breast.
I trembled—and quietly at last
The heaviness of sleep would fall upon my eyes.
Then in a crowd from the blue height,
Winged dreams on a couch of roses,
Sorcerers, enchantresses would fly down
Bewitching my sleep with trickery. . .

Aleksandr's other great comfort at the house in Moscow was his father's French library. Olga observed that her brother was a lazy student, but that he loved reading. He learned mathematics slowly and painfully, but reading and writing came more easily. At the age of nine, he was reading the French translations of the *Iliad* and the *Odyssey,* the great tales of the ancient Greek poet Homer. While reading those books, Aleksandr lived in another world, following the great heroic deeds of Hector and Ajax, or the wonderful sea voyage of the clever trickster Odysseus. He would sneak into his

In the shadows of St. Basil's Cathedral in Moscow, Aleksandr and his servant, Nikita, watched the people going about their daily business.

father's study and read late into the night, or until someone found him there and sent him to bed. His first and lasting favorite writer was the Frenchman Voltaire. Aleksandr quickly memorized many of Voltaire's poems and plays.

Aleksandr's father, Sergey, was not a brilliant man, but he had had a good French education. He wrote a little poetry, as did his brother, Vasily, who was a famous poet during the last years of the 18th century. The Pushkins invited many of Russia's greatest writers to their home. In the evenings, they would sit and talk in Sergey's study. Among the regular guests was the great historian and poet Nikolay Mikhailovich Karamzin. Sergey saw that his son paid close attention to this man. Aleksandr heard Karamzin speak of his warm patriotism, but more importantly he noticed his beautiful use of language. As the evening grew late and the child's bedtime drew near, Aleksandr would try to slip quietly behind a chair, and would sometimes go on listening for hours, unnoticed.

At the age of seven or eight, Aleksandr's personality slowly began to change. He went from being a sad, quiet, and lazy child to being more active and stubborn. He was always getting into trouble and arguing with his mother. During these years, he liked to wander about the town of Moscow with Nikita Timofeyevich Kozlov, Aleksandr's life-long servant. With Nikita, Aleksandr climbed the bell tower of Ivan the Great—tsar from 1462 to 1505. They walked in the shadows of Moscow's great spiral domes. In 1809, they stood together on the steps of Myaznitskaya Church to watch the newly crowned tsar, Alexander I, pass by, followed by the noblemen and soldiers dressed for the parade.

Nikita was Aleksandr's worldly teacher. He led the boy into the crowded little streets and alleys where the common people lived. There, Aleksandr saw people do their daily business, with lively hand gestures and loud voices, with anger and with laughter. He went to the outdoor comedies in which he watched the actions of wealthy fools, mean-spirited landlords, clever cheats, beggars, and simple, happy lovers.

Aleksandr's happiest childhood memories, however, were of the summers spent at his grandmother's country estate in Zakharovo. From 1805 until Napoleon's invasion of Russia in 1812, he spent time in the birch woods where he and his sister and brothers played games with the local peasant children. In the evenings, the village girls danced in a ring. There were country festivals full of songs.

Aleksandr's younger brother, Nikolay, became very sick at Zakharovo in the summer of 1807. During Nikolay's illness, Aleksandr once leaned over his bed to look at him; Nikolay had only enough strength to stick out his tongue in an attempt to make Aleksandr laugh. Soon after, Nikolay died.

At Zakharovo, too, Aleksandr fell in love for the first time. He was nine years old when he met the eight-year-old Sophia Sushkov at a dance lesson. Seven years later, he still thought of her as the "sweet spirit" that haunted the quiet and most beautiful hours of his day.

In July 1811, Aleksandr set out for St. Petersburg to attend a new boarding school on the tsar's estate. His parents had planned to send him to another school, but when they found out about the free education at the new lycée, or government-run high school, they were happy to get rid of their troublesome son for six years. Aleksandr prepared to leave Moscow, Olga and Lev, his grandmother and his nanny, and to start a new life in a new place.

Aleksandr reads in the gardens of the Tsarskoye Selo Lycée.

❧ TWO ❧

To Tsarskoye Selo
1811-1814

Aleksandr arrived in St. Petersburg on July 20, 1811, in the company of his uncle, Vasily Lvovich Pushkin. Unlike hilly Moscow, St. Petersburg was situated on level ground, at the edge of the Baltic Sea. Aleksandr liked the straight avenues that were lined with majestic buildings. There were canals with granite embankments and walkways. The people looked busy and serious.

Upon arrival, Vasily decided to stay at the oldest and most elegant hotel in town. To help pay for the rooms, he "borrowed" from Aleksandr the 100 rubles that the boy's grandmother and aunt had given him, leaving Aleksandr without any spending money during his first months at the lycée.

Vasily looked up some of his literary friends in the city, and during the few weeks before the entrance examinations, Aleksandr went with him to several meetings in which the writers shared their ideas. At that time, there were two groups of writers. On the one side, the Lovers of Russian Letters, led by Aleksandr Semyonovich Shishkov, disapproved of the modern French influence and wanted Russian writers to return to the Slavonic language of the church. The other group, the Arzamas Society of Obscure People, was led by Nikolay Karamzin, Vasily Pushkin, and Vasily Andreyevich Zhukovsky. To the Arzamas writers, the French language and culture stood for knowledge itself. They wanted the freedom to describe the common joys of life including those that the church frowned upon—music, dancing, drinking, and

Nikolay Mikhailovich Karamzin, left, *and Vasily Andreyevich Zhukovsky,* right—*two poets who were a great influence on Aleksandr throughout his life*

general revelry. Aleksandr listened to the Arzamas writers, longing for the day when he could be one of them.

Aleksandr took his lycée examinations in the office of the minister of education on August 12. As the boys and their parents stood in a large hall waiting for the names to be called, Vasily introduced his nephew to one of the other students. The student was Ivan Ivanovich Pushchin, who took an immediate liking to Aleksandr, perhaps because their names sounded alike. Ivan and the "bright, frizzly-headed boy with flickering eyes" soon became best friends. Aleksandr often invited his friend to tea at the hotel, where Vasily's pretty maid would serve them and laughingly return their jokes.

When Aleksandr's name was called, a servant led him to the minister's office, where he stood across the table from the minister himself, who was dressed in full uniform. As the minister looked on, Aleksandr nervously answered the questions of the lycée's headmaster, the tall, angular, good-natured Malinovsky.

Aleksandr passed the examination with the following scores:

Russian grammar:	very good
French grammar:	good
German:	did not study
arithmetic:	knowledge elementary
geography and history:	knowledge elementary

Twenty-nine other students passed, among them Ivan and another boy who would become a close friend of Aleksandr's — Anton Antonovich Delvig, a fellow poet.

The boys moved into their rooms on October 13, and Aleksandr found himself next door to his friend Ivan. Aleksandr described his little room in a poem to his sister:

A latch on the door...
A rickety chair, unupholstered,
And a wobbly bed, a vessel filled with water,
A reed pipe.

He had a small desk, soon to be covered with papers on which he had written poems and ideas for poems.

The lycée was outside of the city, in a wing of Tsarskoye Selo Palace, the tsar's palace. The opening of the new school on October 19 was something of a national event. Tsar Alexander I himself was present to welcome the boys. They stood before him in their new uniforms: blue coats with red collars, white shirts and trousers, boots, and three-cornered hats. The headmaster, Malinovsky, gave a quiet speech, which was followed by a rousing patriotic speech by Professor Kunitsyn. Finally the emperor, in Pushchin's words, "bowed graciously to each of us and patiently received our awkward bows."

The purpose of the lycée was to train "young men destined for high government office, chosen from among the best which the foremost families had to offer." In fact, the foremost, or wealthiest, families wanted to educate their boys at home. But the poorer families of the old nobility, who could not afford private tutors, were glad to send their sons to the lycée, where they would have six years of training with some of the best teachers in Russia.

Each student was given a valet, or personal servant. The servants played an important role in the boys' lives, sometimes even helping them in their pranks. One servant, against the rules, set up a candy shop for the boys. Aleksandr's assigned valet became the most notorious of the servants, for he was found guilty of having committed several murders and robberies during the two years he served Aleksandr. Aleksandr later wrote a poem in which he rejoiced at having escaped his murderous valet.

Within days after the lycée opened, Malinovsky announced that the boys would be forbidden to leave the palace grounds during their six years at the school. Close relatives were permitted to visit on holidays only. The announcement shocked the students. They started to whisper about their new "prison." But classes had begun, and the full schedule kept them busy.

The students got up at 6:00 A.M., attended prayers until 7:00, then lessons until 9:00, followed by breakfast and a group walk until 10:00. After two more hours of class and a

Tsarskoye Selo—the tsar's village—in the early 1800s, when Aleksandr was a student at the lycée

second walk, they ate lunch at 1:00 P.M. This was followed by three hours of class, then tea and a third walk, and then homework. The boys ate dinner at 8:30 and enjoyed an hour of play before bedtime.

Often, after dark, Aleksandr would call across the room divider to Ivan and they would talk about the day's events. At first, Ivan was Aleksandr's only friend. The other boys didn't like Aleksandr because he would insult them and make jokes about them whenever they bothered him. Aleksandr was shy, proud, and also a little afraid. Most of the boys were bigger than he, and some of them were barons or princes. Aleksandr used his cleverness with words as a defense, so that he wouldn't feel inferior to them. Eventually the other boys accepted Aleksandr. They grew used to his sharp tongue, and even learned to laugh at the humor of his jibes. He also learned to like them, especially after discovering that some of them wrote poetry.

In the first few months at Tsarskoye Selo, the students began publishing two papers: the *Tsarskoye Selo School Gazette* and the *Tsarskoye Selo Imperial School Herald.* A number of other papers followed, all of them copied out by hand and passed around among the students. The papers were full of jokes, anecdotes, poems, and cartoons. They often poked fun at teachers and fellow students. Events at the school became the subject of songs, short poems, or drawings.

Poetry writing became so popular among the students that rival groups formed, with Aleksandr, Anton, and Pyotr Aleksandrovich Korsakov publishing *The Inexperienced Pen,* and Vilgelm Karlovich Kyukhelbeker and Mikhail

Tsarskoye Selo Imperial School Herald —*published by the students at Tsarskoye Selo*

подарокъ отъ № 7

Императорскаго Сарско-
сельскаго Лицея.

Вѣстникъ № 1й

3го Декабря 1811го Года

29го Ноября Лицей.

Мы получили извѣстіе о весьма страстныхъ произшествій случившееся въ теченіе сего мѣсяца, и мы посмышляемъ увѣдомлять объ нихъ нашу почтеннѣйшую публику.

28 Ноября. Ночь физическій залъ

извѣстно всѣмъ вражда которая завелась между Княземъ Горчаковымъ Гмъ Масловымъ и Гмъ Ламоносовымъ. Мы уже отчаявали видѣть прежде согласіе, какъ сего дня Князь Горчаковъ видя что одное самолюбіе заставляло соперниковъ его не предполагать примиреніе, послалъ Гна Гребеницу правителя секретной Экспедиціи доложить Гну Маслову что онъ желаетъ съ нимъ имѣть поговоръ и какъ скоро Масловъ пришелъ Князь ему сказалъ, Милостивой Государь сказалъ онъ я за бы уваженіе хотя ненавижу васъ столь долѣе время радъ какъ я думаю что лучше вредитъ нашей произшедшіи раздоры, предлагаю вамъ миръ, Гнъ Масловъ тронный силъ великихъ поступомъ великодушно заключилъ сіи миръ въ скоре послѣ, Гнъ Ламоносовъ прекратилъ свои гнѣвы и теперь сіи три знатные особи бываютъ что въ мѣстѣ и тишина нашъ возстановленъ.

29го Ноября отъ туда – же

Мы получили нѣкоторое весьма любопытныя письма изъ секретной Экспедиціи они писаны на францусскомъ языкѣ.

1е Письмо

Гна Барона Гребеница къ Князю Горчакову

Могу ли я узнать причину вашей холодности со мною? Вашъ сердечный другъ С—ла также не хочетъ быть со мною и я совсѣмъ не знаю причину сего.

Подписано
Баронъ Гребеницъ

II. Письмо

Отвѣтъ Князя Горчакова.

Я не знаю находите ли вы меня вашимъ непріятелемъ но что касается до С—ла я прочту его добрыхъ манеровъ.

Подписано
Князь Горчаковъ

Мы письма жалѣемъ что немогли доставить протчихъ писемъ Гна Ламоносова Гну Гребеницу и Князю Горчакову. Но въ будущемъ нумерѣ мы постараемся ихъ доставить.

Сіи извѣстіе нами собрано въ Горсаковскихъ. Издатель Сарскосельскій Лицейскихъ Газетъ. № 1.

Lukianovich Yakovlev publishing *For Pleasure and Profit*. Aleksandr and his fellow poets at Tsarskoye Selo were excited about poetry because they realized that they stood at the forefront of the movement to write literature in the Russian language. French literature belonged to a very old tradition, but the Russian tradition was just beginning to take shape; the direction it would take would depend on the creativity of the younger poets.

The new headmaster, Piletsky, taking note of the boys' love of poetry, decided to sponsor a society for future poets. The students liked the idea so much that many were soon spending their free time at the library reading and writing poetry. They would even write poems in class rather than listen to the teachers or do their work. Piletsky, believing that the students had gotten out of hand, reacted by forbidding them to write any verses at all. But it was too late. They went on writing in secret and would whisper their poems to one another in class or during walks.

Aleksandr himself was a marvel to the other boys. They admired him for his knowledge and great memory of the French classics, but they were also proud to know this boy who had grown up in the presence of Russia's greatest living writers—especially Zhukovsky and Karamzin. Aleksandr, on the other hand, never bragged about his abilities or his connections. He often seemed more interested in games than in poetry. He hated to lose. Pushchin described him as lost in thought at one moment, and, at the next moment, challenging his fellow students to a footrace.

One classmate described the way Aleksandr wrote poetry: "Ideas for poems came to him, not only during his free periods or when he was out walking, but also in class, and even in church." He would suddenly smile or frown and would nervously bite his fingernails as he wrote. Then, with "his eyes of fire," he would read to himself in a low voice what he had just written.

The boys were fond of singing and sometimes made up tunes to sing with their poetry. Pyotr, who played the guitar, and Mikhail, who played the violin, set some of Aleksandr's songs to music. The boys also had story-telling contests, which Aleksandr loved. Anton was the best, however, because he was a great liar and would tell stories about wars he claimed to have seen with his own eyes.

The boys all loved Professor Galich, the teacher of Russian literature, who encouraged their poetic strivings even when Piletsky forbade the writing of verse. Galich's classes were long, freewheeling discussions in which the students could talk about whatever interested them. The students thought of Galich as a lovable scatterbrain. Years later, Aleksandr referred to him as a man who "encouraged me in my chosen path."

Professor Kunitsyn, the philosophy teacher, was another favorite. He openly condemned serfdom, a system in which peasants are bound to work on the land for the nobility. He taught his students about the natural rights of all people. His effect on them was profound in terms of the political views that many of them would attempt to put into practice. Ten years later, in 1821, he was forced to quit his job because of his liberal views. Aleksandr wrote in his poem *October 19, 1825:*

> To Kunitsyn, our hearts and glasses raise,
> He modeled us, he breathed upon our coals.

The boys had liked their soft-hearted first headmaster, Malinovsky. His replacement, Piletsky, they hated. Not only was Piletsky a stickler for every rule, but he also had the mean habit of punishing the rule-breakers by making them kneel on the hard stone floor of the chapel during prayers. Moreover, he had the bad manners to be rude to the students' mothers and sisters during their school visits. By the end of 1813, the students could bear the headmaster no longer, and they plotted to get rid of him. They achieved their goal when Aleksandr stood up at a house dinner and recited a list of Piletsky's "crimes." The teachers became furious and forced Piletsky to leave the school.

Almost every teacher's report on Aleksandr's progress at the lycée described him as "brilliant rather than thorough." He was capable of outshining the other pupils, especially when there was a contest and he set his mind to the task. But

The young poet in 1817

usually he wrote poems, drew pictures, daydreamed, and neglected his studies in general. His real education came from watching the way people acted, listening to the best teachers, and endlessly reading and writing.

During the first few years Aleksandr was at the lycée, his father had been stationed far away in Warsaw. Sergey did not visit his son until he moved to St. Petersburg in October 1814. By that time, Aleksandr had already gotten himself into trouble. One month before his father's visit, the new headmaster, Hauenschild, had noticed a number of students behaving strangely at dinner. He had discovered that they were drunk. When he had demanded to know what had happened, Aleksandr, Ivan, and Ivan Vasilyevich Malinovsky had stood up to take the blame.

Earlier that day, Aleksandr had gotten a bottle of rum from a servant and used it to mix a strong punch called "gogelmogel." The three boys had then invited other students to a party in one of their rooms, where they drank too much and became rowdy. Aleksandr was proud of this party and even wrote a poem celebrating it. Such "adventures," often led by Aleksandr and his friends, were common enough, but this time the boys were almost kicked out of school. Aleksandr's father probably spoke with him about the incident, but the talk had little effect on Aleksandr's behavior, for he continued his mischief.

Aleksandr at the lycée

❧ THREE ❧

The Bright-Eyed
Young Rebel

1815-1820

It was Professor Galich who suggested that Aleksandr write his long poem *Recollections of Tsarskoye Selo* for the public examination of 1815. The great old poet Gavrila Romanovich Derzhavin promised to attend the ceremonies. The students were excited. Anton Delvig waited in the entrance hall, planning to greet the poet by kissing his hand. However, when Derzhavin entered, he immediately asked the doorman where the toilets were. This everyday question spoiled the magic of the moment for Anton who decided to return to his seat in the examination hall.

"I saw Derzhavin only once in my life," wrote Aleksandr, "but I shall never forget the occasion." Derzhavin looked very old. The examination seemed to tire him very much until the section on Russian literature began. Then he "came to life, his eyes shone; he was completely transformed." The students were reading his verses, analyzing them, praising them.

"At last I was called. I recited my *Recollections of Tsarskoye Selo* while standing three feet away from Derzhavin." When Aleksandr reached the lines that mention Derzhavin, he could hardly hold back his joy. "My youthful voice rang and my heart throbbed," Aleksandr recalled. Derzhavin listened with a surprised smile on his face. Once the examinations had ended, Derzhavin demanded to see the bright-eyed poet whose verse had made him feel young again; he wanted to embrace him. They looked for Aleksandr but could not find him. The young poet had fled the room, overcome by excitement.

Later that day, at a dinner at which Sergey Pushkin was present, the minister of education suggested that Aleksandr

At the public exams in 1815, Aleksandr recited his poem,
Recollections of Tsarskoye Selo.

*Gavrila Romanovich
Derzhavin*

should be taught to write other things besides poetry. Derzhavin turned red and insisted, "Leave him as he is: a poet!" Derzhavin sat and read several other poems by Pushkin. He paused, then said, "This is the one who will take Derzhavin's place."

The examination of 1815 marked the beginning of Pushkin's national fame as a poet. His *Recollections of Tsarskoye Selo* was published in the April issue of the *Russian Museum*. This poem — which described the lycee and the gardens of the palace, and told of the burning of Moscow and the Russian victory over Napoleon in 1812 — was not a great poem. Its style was a little old-fashioned. Nevertheless, its rhythm and language were handled with a sureness and beauty very rare for a 15-year-old poet. The editors of the *Russian Museum* —

one of the best critical reviews of the day — wrote that the poet's talent showed "great promise." Anton sent many of Aleksandr's poems to magazines, and by September 1815, Aleksandr was the author of 20 published poems.

In September, the poet Vasily Zhukovsky, then at the height of his fame, wrote a letter to his friend Pyotr Andreyevich Vyazemsky after meeting "our young miracle worker Pushkin" at Tsarskoye Selo. "He is the hope of our literary club," he wrote. "The only thing that I am afraid of is that, imagining himself to be mature, he may keep himself from growing to maturity. We must all unite in helping this future giant to grow up. He will outstrip us all."

The "future giant" was still, in many respects, very much a boy. In his diary on December 10, 1815, Aleksandr noted that he wrote the third chapter of a long philosophical poem, read it to a fellow student, and then in the evening ran through the hallway with his classmates putting out all the candles and lamps. Perfectly aware of his childishness, he laughed at himself, calling the hallway prank "an excellent activity for a philosopher."

Zhukovsky was concerned about Pushkin's education. He believed that a German university would be best. Aleksandr, however, was not interested in school. He continued to do well in Russian and French literature, but he was at the bottom of his class in every other subject. He devoted his time to poetry. He wrote 26 poems in 1814, 27 in 1815, and over 50 in 1816.

Meanwhile, he was meeting with many of Russia's older poets when they visited the school. In May 1816, Karamzin moved to Tsarskoye Selo. He visited the school and, according to a classmate, told Aleksandr to "soar like an eagle, but do not falter in your flight."

At the beginning of 1816, the new headmaster, Engel-hardt, changed some school rules, allowing the students to go to parties and take walks beyond the school grounds. This new freedom permitted Aleksandr to spend many hours at the Karamzins'. Discussions and arguments with the great historian formed a major part of Aleksandr's education during his last years at the lycée.

At the Karamzins', Aleksandr would tell stories, make jokes and laugh loudly. Sometimes Nikolay Karamzin would look at him sternly to let him know he was being a little too loud. Aleksandr liked to listen to Karamzin when he spoke of Russian history, but he disagreed with Karamzin's political views.

Once, when Karamzin was explaining to Aleksandr the reasons for keeping serfs in Russia, Aleksandr challenged him with the question, "So you prefer slavery to freedom, do you?" Karamzin was embarrassed and accused Aleksandr of slandering him. Aleksandr "said nothing, respecting the anger of a beautiful soul. We changed the subject." Soon Karamzin felt sorry. As he said good-bye to Aleksandr, he blamed him in such a way that Aleksandr understood it as an apology as well. "You said something to me today which none of my enemies would ever have said to me."

These discussions and arguments were only one side of their friendship. Beneath the seriousness, both men saw the humor of their opposing personalities. "Once on his way to the Palace in Pavlovsk," Aleksandr remembered, "he cast a sidelong glance at me as he was putting on his sash and could not help laughing. I guffawed and both of us burst into loud laughter."

Aleksandr also went to the Karamzins' for the purpose of seeing Nikolay's wife, Yekaterina Andreyevna Karamzin.

Nikolay Mikhailovich and Yekaterina Andreyevna Karamzin

At 36 years old, the lovely Yekaterina was 19 years older than Aleksandr. She received a love letter from Aleksandr and showed it to her husband. The Karamzins decided to treat the matter with kindness. Aleksandr's love amused Yekaterina. She also seemed to sense that he was searching for someone to replace a mother who never loved him. They became friends and remained close until Aleksandr's death.

The headmaster, Engelhardt, held dances and parties at his home. There, and at the other houses, the students could meet and dance with the daughters of the local nobility. The students also met soldiers, the hussar, or Russian cavalry, officers who were stationed in Tsarskoye Selo. This new social life was important for Pushkin's growth as a poet. He heard the officers tell of the wars and of the behavior of soldiers under fire. At the parties and dinners, he observed the loves, passions, and vanities of the people around him.

He himself fell in love often and was aware of his own trouble-some vanity, his desire to be seen and heard, to have people admire him and laugh at his jokes.

At the Karamzins' house, Aleksandr met the hussar guardsman Pyotr Yakovlevich Chaadayev, who introduced him to General Nikolay Nikolayevich Raevsky and other officers. Chaadayev and Raevsky were heroes of the war against Napoleon. They, along with many of their fellow officers, were liberals who wanted to free the serfs and to limit the tsar's power.

Pushkin, Pushchin, and several other students in their late teens spent much of their free time with the hussars, sometimes staying out all night talking, drinking, and playing cards. Pushchin remembered that their talks with the hussars dealt with "social problems and the evils of the existing order of things and the possibility of changing it. Pushkin always agreed with their ideas and in his own way expressed them in his poems and prose." It is hard to say what attracted Aleksandr most, the liberal discussions or the card playing, for Pushkin was addicted to gambling.

Pushkin's friendship with the hussars encouraged him to think about joining the cavalry. He pictured himself riding through the fiery battlefields holding a sword in one hand and twirling his handsome moustache with the other, for cavalrymen always wore moustaches. Aleksandr's graduation was approaching and he wrote to his family to convince them that a military career would be best for him. However, by the time he had passed his final examinations in May 1817, he had decided to devote all of his energy to poetry. He graduated from the lycée with the lowest rank in the civil service and was given a paid position, but no real work to do, in the Ministry of Foreign Affairs.

While still a student, Aleksandr had received two com-
missions, or paid requests, to write poems. The first came
from the minister of education, who asked for a poem celebrating the tsar's return from Paris in 1815. Aleksandr completed the poem and hoped that Tsar Alexander himself would
read it, but the poem never reached the tsar. Pushkin was
seeking the official attention that had once been Derzhavin's
and was now enjoyed by Zhukovsky.

In 1816, a second commission followed, with better results. An old court poet had been asked to write a long poem
to celebrate the wedding of the grand duchess Anna
Pavlovna. He felt unable to write the poem in such a rush,
so Karamzin suggested that the poet offer the commission to
Pushkin. Aleksandr accepted the offer and finished on time.
His poem was sung at the wedding reception. It pleased
Tsarina Maria Fyodorovna, Paul I's wife, so much that she
sent Pushkin a gold watch.

Aleksandr spent the summer after his graduation at
Mikhailovskoye, his mother's country estate. In August 1817,
he returned to St. Petersburg and took a small room at his
parents' apartments, a room he described as "cramped and
simple." He seldom had money, and when he did, he would
quickly gamble it away. Then he would have to borrow from
his father, who never lent to him without complaining.

Aleksandr lived a double life in St. Petersburg. He loved
the nightlife. He attended dances and went to the theatre.
He amazed his friends with the energy he had to stay out
late drinking and playing cards night after night. But he also
spent many hours at home in his room writing poetry. Card
games were a passion with him, but poetry was his first love.

In 1817, his last year at the lycée, Aleksandr had begun a
long poem, *Ruslan and Lyudmila*. He didn't finish it until the

spring of 1820. The poem tells the story of the brave knight Ruslan, who travels in search of the lovely princess Lyudmila, who has been kidnapped by an evil magician. After many hardships, Ruslan defeats the magician and marries Lyudmila. Instead of being like the gloomy romances of Zhukovsky, *Ruslan and Lyudmila* is closer to the lively spirit of Russian folktales. Also, the style of the poem is close to common Russian speech. Zhukovsky saw that Pushkin had begun to outshine him. After Pushkin read the poem at Zhukovsky's on March 26, 1820, the older poet gave Pushkin a portrait of himself, on which he had written, "To the victorious pupil from the conquered teacher."

The publishing of *Ruslan and Lyudmila* caused an uproar. Many of the older poets and critics hated it. In the magazines, they wrote that the language was low and unpoetic, and that the tale had no moral lesson. The public and most of the younger poets loved it. Pushkin's popularity grew. Earlier poets had been chosen by the tsar, but Aleksandr Pushkin was the first poet to be chosen by the people.

Pushkin also became famous for fighting in duels — formal combats between two people, fought with weapons and in the presence of witnesses. It seems, however, that no one was ever killed in these duels. Aleksandr himself was usually responsible for these showdowns, for his jokes were often taken as insults. In addition, once he had provoked someone to speak harshly in reaction, he was very sensitive to any statement touching his honor.

One evening, Pushkin was making catcalls in the theatre and an army officer complained because he couldn't hear the actors. Pushkin continued to groan and whistle. In the aisle after the play, the officer stopped Pushkin and, pointing his finger, told him he had behaved rudely. The pointing angered Pushkin, who quickly challenged the officer to a duel. The officer didn't wish to duel with a young man he had never seen before. When it later became clear that this young man was the poet Aleksandr Pushkin, the officer decided to apologize rather than fight a duel that could only be embarrassing to both of them.

On another occasion, Vilgelm Karlovich Kyukhelbeker, Pushkin's old school friend, became so upset by some lines Pushkin wrote making fun of his poetry that he challenged Pushkin to a duel. Kyukhelbeker shot first and missed. Then Pushkin laughed and threw away his pistol, refusing to fire back. Kyukhelbeker screamed at him to shoot, but Pushkin told him that the barrel of the pistol was now full of snow.

Pushkin joined the Arzamas Society of Obscure People. The younger writers, including Pushkin, believed that the Arzamas should have a political purpose. The older writers, among them Karamzin and Zhukovsky, supported the tsar and wanted to keep Russia the way it was. This disagreement led to the breakup of the group. By the end of 1818, the younger writers, led by Yakov Tolstoy, had launched their own poetry society. They called it the Green Lamp, after the lamp that hung in their meeting room.

The Green Lamp was a writers' club, a drinking club, and an association of young rebels. It lasted for two years, when the police began to arrest people at all meetings not approved by the tsar. Some political groups continued to meet in secret to plot an overthrow of the tsar's government. Many of Pushkin's friends were members, but they would not discuss their plans with Pushkin. Pushchin explained that Pushkin talked too much and had too many friends who could not be trusted. Keeping these secrets from Pushkin

Aleksandr Ivanovich Turgenev, one of the brothers who challenged Pushkin to write Ode to Liberty

protected the political societies and saved Pushkin, as well. But Pushkin got into trouble of his own.

Among the members of the Green Lamp were Pushkin, Delvig, and the Turgenev brothers—Aleksandr Ivanovich and Nikolay Ivanovich. In December 1817, the Turgenevs challenged Pushkin to write a poem about the Mikhailovsky Palace. They said they were tired of Pushkin's love poems and wanted to see him write about freedom. Laughing, Pushkin agreed to the challenge and started writing.

Mikhailovsky Palace could be seen from the window of Nikolay Turgenev's room. It had been left empty by Tsar Alexander I after his father, Paul I, was murdered there. The poem Pushkin wrote, *Ode to Liberty,* is a warning to the leaders of all countries that they are in danger of being put to death if they do not give their people more freedom. One passage describes the death of Louis XVI of France, whose head was cut off in 1793 during the French Revolution. Another describes the murder of Paul I. The poem closes with a demand

In Ode to Liberty, *Pushkin wrote of the murder of Tsar Paul I.*

for emperors and kings to bow their heads to common law. "You stand higher than the nation, but the eternal Law is higher than you." What Pushkin's poem demands is a constitution, or a set of laws, to be written by educated men to limit the power of the tsar.

The poem was dangerous because it made a threat on the life of the tsar and because it reminded the people of a rumor that Alexander I had helped plan his father's murder. When this poem and others of its kind reached the hands of the tsar, Pushkin was in danger of punishment.

Tsar Alexander I wanted to exile, or banish, Pushkin from his home to the distant, cold land of Siberia. Several of Pushkin's friends, including Chaadayev, pleaded for Pushkin. The tsar met Pushkin's old headmaster, Engelhardt, in the park of the lycée and told him what he planned to do. Engelhardt, who thought that life in Siberia might destroy Pushkin, asked the tsar to be merciful and convinced him that his kindness was "much more likely to put some sense" into Pushkin's head.

On May 6, 1820, Pushkin was forced to leave St. Petersburg. He was sent on a hard, 10-day journey by coach to the small southern town of Yekaterinoslav. There he was assigned to the office of General Ivan Nikitich Inzov, who governed the southern Russian colonies. Although Pushkin knew he was being punished, he tried to think of his exile as a lucky escape from St. Petersburg.

*Aleksandr called his travels to the Caucasus with the Raevskys
"the happiest moments" of his life.*

➤ FOUR ❖

Exiled to the South

1820-1824

Before leaving St. Petersburg, Pushkin had learned of a false rumor. People had begun saying that he had been brought before the police and whipped because of his poems against the tsar. The poet had been outraged by this insult to his nobility. In his mind, he had seen all of society laughing at him. He became so angry he had wanted to kill one of his enemies. That way, he really would have been sent to Siberia.

Only Delvig and one other friend had gone with him to the station at Tsarskoye Selo to see him on his way. Now he was traveling out of the foggy city and into the open country-side. In St. Petersburg, he drank too much, argued too much, gambled too much. He was continually becoming ill. His friends reported that he did most of his writing during his illnesses, when he couldn't move from his bed. They hoped he would find more time to write in the south.

Aleksandr arrived in Yekaterinoslav in mid-May and reported to General Inzov. After arriving there he wrote to his brother Lev, "I became bored, I went boating on the Dneper River and took a swim, and I caught a fever as usual. General Raevsky, who was on his way to the Caucasus with a son and two daughters, found me in a Jewish hut, with a fever and no doctor, a pitcher of iced lemonade beside me."

General Raevsky's second son, Nikolay Nikolayevich, asked Aleksandr if he would like to go with the Raevskys to the mineral baths in the Caucasus Mountains between the Black Sea and the Caspian Sea. Aleksandr made the Raevskys' doctor promise not to starve him to death on the way. Then he got permission from General Inzov. Inzov was now in charge of teaching Pushkin to be a better citizen. He knew, however, that the young man was unhappy in such a small town and that it would do no good to keep him there. He put the poet

General Nikolay
Nikolayevich Raevsky,
a hero of the war
against Napoleon

in the care of General Raevsky, then wrote to the tsar explaining his decision. Aleksandr stayed with the Raevskys from the beginning of June until late September 1820. They spent two months in the Caucasus Mountains. This region was newly conquered by Russia. Scattered troops of Circassians were still fighting the cossacks, the Russian cavalry. The Raevskys traveled with 60 armed guards and a loaded cannon.

Aleksandr was sick when the journey began, but was soon well and enjoying the mountain air. He wrote to Lev: "I'm sorry, my friend, that you could not see this magnificent range of mountains, with their icy summits, which from afar in the clear twilight look like strange, many-colored and motionless clouds. I am sorry that you could not climb with me to the sharp peak of five-ridged Beshtu, of Mashuk and Iron Stone and Serpent mountains."

He called his days with the Raevskys "the happiest moments" of his life. General Raevsky was almost like a father to him. He found the daughters "charming," and he especially liked the oldest son, Aleksandr Nikolayevich.

Aleksandr Nikolayevich Raevsky was four years older than Aleksandr Pushkin. He was a thin, sarcastic young man, who seemed to Aleksandr to be wiser than his years. Aleksandr remained captivated by him for several years, and the two young men became close friends. Raevsky read Aleksandr's poems and made fun of his beliefs. He himself seemed to believe in nothing. In his view, the world was filled with selfish and stupid people who deserved only scorn. Although it was Nikolay Raevsky who introduced Aleksandr to the poetry of Byron, it was his brother, Aleksandr Raevsky, who most resembled a Byronic hero. George Gordon, Lord Byron—who lived a romantic, adventurous life—was the most famous English poet of the day. Like many young men in Europe who read Byron's poems, Aleksandr Raevsky imitated the Byronic hero, who mocked society's belief in religion, morality, and love.

Aleksandr stayed at the Raevskys' estate in Gurzuf, at the edge of the Black Sea in the Crimea. The Crimea, with its sea cliffs, its Roman ruins, its grapes, valley streams, and poplar trees, was a delight. There Aleksandr fell in love with the 22-year-old Yekaterina Nikolayevna Raevsky, the family beauty. Pushkin addressed several love poems to her during his month at Gurzuf. When an editor published two of these poems in 1824 without Pushkin's permission, the poet became angry. He didn't want to embarrass Yekaterina, who had since married General Mikhail Fyodorovich Orlov. He admitted that he "happened once to be madly in love" with

In 1820, Aleksandr learned about the romantic poet George Gordon, Lord Byron from his friend Aleksandr Raevsky. Like Byron, Pushkin wanted to live a romantic, adventurous life.

*Yekaterina
Nikolayevna
Raevsky*

her and was afraid now that, if she were to read the poems, she would think he had talked about her with all of his St. Petersburg friends. "I confess," he wrote, "that I value one thought of that woman more than the opinions of all the journals in the world and of our entire public."

Pushkin was sad to leave the Raevskys in September to return to the offices of General Inzov, but he soon found a way of seeing them again. General Inzov had moved his headquarters to Kishinev, some 90 miles (145 kilometers) northwest of Odessa. Kishinev had recently been under Turkish rule. The men wore beards and turbans. Aleksandr loved the native Moldavian folk songs and dances. He liked to break away suddenly from his surprised friends and join in the dances of the local people. But in a town of fewer than ten families of Russian nobility, he was soon bored with the social life. Fortunately, he was invited to the birthday party of General Raevsky's mother, Yekaterina Davydov, in Kamenka. Aleksandr left Kishinev in mid-November with the promise to return in two weeks, but he ended up staying in Kamenka until March.

For several years, the birthday parties of Yekaterina Davydov had been the occasion for secret meetings among the radical military officers who wished to overthrow the tsarist government. Pushkin himself suspected that a secret society existed. He wished to be a part of it, but the members knew that he talked too much and would be likely, in a fit of anger, to blurt out an important secret to an enemy.

Ivan Yakushkin, General Mikhail Orlov, and Orlov's secretary, Konstantin Alekseyevich Okhotnikov, were leaders of the secret society called the Union of Welfare. They planned to overthrow the tsar and set up a constitutional government. They were meeting at the Davydovs' to organize a large conference of rebels to be held in Moscow in January 1821. General Raevsky, although not a member, seemed to guess what was going on. On the last evening of the meeting, the leaders decided to confuse Raevsky with a trick. They held a formal meeting and asked him to be the chair. They were to discuss whether creating a secret society would be a good thing.

Pushkin said that he was very much in favor. Yakushkin argued against him. Then General Raevsky named all the cases in which a secret society could act with success and be of benefit. Yakushkin replied: "I can easily prove to you that you are not serious about this. Let me ask you this question: If there were such a secret society, would you have joined it or not?" Raevsky said that he certainly would have. "In that case," said Yakushkin, "give me your hand." When Raevsky held out his hand, offering to join the society, Yakushkin burst out laughing and said that it was all a joke.

Everyone else laughed except Pushkin, "who was very excited. He had been convinced that the society already existed or was about to be created that very evening and that he would be one of its members. But when he saw that the whole thing was a joke, he stood up, red in the face, and said with tears in his eyes, 'I have never been so unhappy as I am now. I was ready to see my life ennobled and a great purpose set before me, and the whole thing was nothing but a bad joke.'"

Pushkin was ready to throw himself into the conspiracy against the tsar. Like Byron — who traveled to Greece to fight in the war for independence from the Turks — Pushkin wanted to act on his ideas, not just write about them. But no matter how many times he would praise liberty in his poems, his friends in the secret societies, including Pushchin, would always see him as merely a poet. He was a troublemaker and had some right ideas, but he was not a rebel.

While still at Kamenka, Pushkin finished his poem *The Prisoner of the Caucasus*. It is about a Russian who is captured by Circassian warriors. A young Circassian woman falls in love with him and cuts his chains. He, however, is hopelessly in love with another woman. Despite his continuing love for the other woman, he asks the Circassian to flee with him. She refuses, knowing that he will never love her. He swims across the river and escapes. As he is climbing the opposite bank of the river, he hears a splash on the other side. He realizes that the Circassian, true to her passionate spirit, has drowned herself out of grief.

Pushkin sold his poems. It was his great discovery that he could earn a living by writing. No Russian writer had

The great poet in exile

ever done so before. The only problem was that his censors, the tsar's officers in charge of reading and approving works to be published, often cut out lines and changed sentences. People were eager to buy Pushkin's works, but he was not eager to publish, when he knew the censors might destroy the meaning of his poems.

On Pushkin's return to Kishinev, General Inzov continued to look after him like a father. Whenever the tsar wrote asking about Pushkin's behavior, General Inzov replied that the poet was behaving very properly. The truth was, however, that Pushkin had been speaking out against the government in the general's home and at local cafés. He had been put under house arrest twice, for insulting a military officer and for slapping a local landowner. He gambled.

Aleksandr was sent to the city of Odessa in 1823.

He fought in perhaps a dozen duels. He was known to dress up in Moldavian and Turkish costumes, to speak in foreign accents, and generally to behave like a clown in public.

Such behavior perhaps showed his frustration with being so far away from his friends and from the social life of St. Petersburg. He complained that none of his old friends ever wrote to him. He wanted them to plead with the tsar to call him back to St. Petersburg.

Then, when he wasn't expecting it, his friends Pyotr Vyazemsky and Aleksandr Turgenev got him an appointment in Odessa in the offices of Count Mikhail Semyonovich Vorontsov, the new governor-general of southern Russia. Aleksandr arrived in Odessa in July 1823. Although smaller than St. Petersburg, Odessa was a large town with a cosmopolitan style of life. Even though Aleksandr complained about the roads turning to dust in the summer and to thick mud in the winter, there were theatres, dances, drinking parties, and gambling in Odessa. These new activities greatly raised

Aleksandr's spirits. At the same time, however, they drove him into debt. His salary was low and he no longer had free rooms as he had had at Kishinev. Soon he was writing home to Lev, asking him to "explain to my father that I cannot live without some money from him." He refused to sell his poems if they were going to be ruined by the censors.

Finally he did sell *The Fountain of Bakhchisaray* to a Moscow dealer for 3,000 rubles. This was enough to live on for a time. He paid most of his debts. But trouble was approaching from another direction.

For some time, he had been in love with the Countess Elizaveta Ksaveryevna Vorontsov, and so had his friend Aleksandr Raevsky. Raevsky kept his own love secret, and in order to get rid of his rival, suggested to Elizaveta's husand, Count Vorontsov, that he send Pushkin to fight the locusts that were beginning to destroy crops in the south. Pushkin refused to go and threatened to resign. He wrote a portrait of his false friend Raevsky in his poem *The Demon,* in which he speaks of the "cold poison" that Raevsky had poured into his soul. Pushkin wanted a new appointment. While he waited for an answer from St. Petersburg, Vorontsov was waiting to catch Pushkin in a mistake.

Pushkin was usually careful about the letters he mailed to his friends because he suspected that they were being read by government spies. But he wasn't so careful in a letter he wrote to Kyukhelbeker early in 1824. He wrote that he was "taking lessons in pure atheism," the belief that God does not exist, from an English friend. When this blasphemous letter was opened by the police, Pushkin's fate was sealed. He was forced to leave Odessa on July 31, 1824. He was sent to his family's estate in Mikhailovskoye, far from the high society of St. Petersburg.

A document calling for
Aleksandr's arrest, and
Aleksandr in exile

Aleksandr's self-portrait from the manuscript of Evgeni Onegin

⤷ FIVE ⤶

The Prisoner
of Mikhailovskoye
1824-1826

Pushkin's journey to Mikhailovskoye was long and, for the most part, lonely. He did meet a student from Tsarskoye Selo at a hotel in Chernigov and, in Mogilev, an army officer who was the nephew of his former headmaster, Engelhardt. The student at first mistook Pushkin for a hotel waiter because of his worn and crumpled clothing, but was amazed when he realized he was talking to his hero, the great poet. The army officer gave a party in Pushkin's honor. Otherwise, the 1,000-mile (1,609-km) journey to Mikhailovskoye was dull. The drivers had been ordered to pass through Kiev without stopping at the home of the Raevskys.

The coach finally made its way past the Svyatogorsk Monastery and through the pine forests that surrounded his mother's estate. Aleksandr found his whole family at home — even Lev, who had just been expelled from Tsarskoye Selo. The official reason for his being kicked out was that he was doing poorly in his studies. It is more likely, however, that he was the leader of a group of students who were defending Kyukhelbeker, the Russian teacher. Aleksandr's old friend Kyukhelbeker was in trouble for speaking out against the government.

Aleksandr's father greeted him kindly. However, Sergey was worried that his family was sinking into disgrace. His son had been exiled. The same thing was going to happen to him, Sergey kept saying over and over. He was eager to show the tsar's officers that the father of the rebel was not himself a rebel. He therefore agreed to spy on Aleksandr — to watch his actions, to listen to his speech and report any dangerous statements, and even to open his mail. Meanwhile, he worked hard to find a new official job for Aleksandr.

Aleksandr was silent at first and did his best to get around Sergey. Above all, he couldn't stand to have his father read his mail. His anger grew during three long months until it finally exploded in late October. The first time he tried to complain to his father, his father became angry and wouldn't listen. Aleksandr wrote to Zhukovsky: "I bowed, mounted a horse and rode off. My father called my brother and ordered him to have nothing to do 'with this monster, this unnatural son' (think of my position, Zhukovsky, and be the judge). My head seethed with rage. I went to my father, found him with my mother and told him everything I had been holding back for the last three months. I ended by saying that I was talking to him for the last time. Taking advantage of the fact that no one was there to see, my father rushed out of the room and declared to the whole house that 'I had hit him, wanted to strike him, had raised my hand to him, could have thrashed him.'"

To strike one's father was a serious crime. Although Aleksandr never did hit his father, Sergey's word alone would have been enough to send him to prison. But the matter was soon dropped. It was not, however, forgotten. Aleksandr couldn't forgive his father. They were never truly friendly toward one another again.

Olga and Lev went to St. Petersburg in early November. Their parents soon followed, leaving Aleksandr alone with his boredom. During the day he rode his horse through the countryside. In the evening he listened to his old nanny Arina tell fairy tales. She was his one companion at Mikhailovskoye, his only friend. He loved the fairy tales. For once, it seemed that he was learning something useful. "How wonderful these fairy tales are! Each one is a poem."

Aleksandr reads to his old nanny, Arina Rodionovna, at Mikhailovskoye.

At Mikhailovskoye, Aleksandr wrote a large part of Evgeni Onegin, *the play* Boris Godunov, *and many poems.*

When the snows of winter came on, he was unable to go riding. Instead, he sat at his desk and wrote poetry. Aleksandr had brought with him from Odessa the first pages of his most famous poem, *Evgeni Onegin*—also called *Eugene Onegin*. He had begun to write the poem in Kishinev in May 1823, and he didn't finish it until 1831. Sometimes he would set it aside to work on other poems, but he continued to think about it during those eight years, planning it and changing it.

The final version of *Evgeni Onegin* is divided into 8 cantos, or chapters, of about 50 stanzas each. Each stanza has 14 lines. The main story concerns Evgeni Onegin, a man

In the opening scene of Pyotr Ilich Tchaikovsky's opera Evgeni Onegin, *peasants celebrate at Tatyana's family estate after the harvest, before Tatyana meets Evgeni and falls in love.*

of the world, and Tatyana, an innocent young woman who falls in love with him. Evgeni has left the busy city to find rest at his country estate. There, he dines with Tatyana and her family. She falls in love with him because he seems stormy and romantic, different from the other men she sees in the country. She sends Evgeni a letter telling him of her love, then waits nervously for his reply. Finally he visits and meets her in the garden, where he tells her that he cannot marry her. He says that his heart has grown tired of love and that the coldness of his soul will only make her unhappy. When

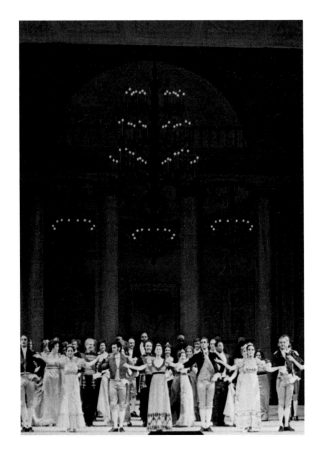

In the third act of Evgeni Onegin, *Evgeni falls in love with Tatyana at a ball in St. Petersburg.*

he sees her years later at a ball in St. Petersburg, she is married to a famous general. She is now Princess Tatyana, an experienced, graceful woman. Now it is his turn to fall in love with her. He goes to balls simply to see her. But she ignores him. In despair, he writes her a love letter. When she doesn't answer, he visits her house. There, she tells him that she loves him still, but that it is too late. She will be faithful to her husband.

In January 1824, Aleksandr wrote to his brother, "It is my finest work." He had written only two cantos. At Mikhailovskoye he completed four more. He also wrote a tragic play, *Boris Godunov,* and several long narrative poems, as well as many short lyrics.

In Modest Mussorgsky's opera Boris Godunov, *Boris—filled with foreboding—prays to God for a blessing during the coronation scene.*

Aleksandr's only nearby friends were his neighbors at the Trigorskoye estate. Everyone there liked him. For him, there were young women to dance with, but the person he really enjoyed was their mother, Praskovia Aleksandrovna Osipov. The others, he felt, were fools, and he wondered how his sister Olga could stand them.

Two visits from old friends broke Aleksandr's boredom. Ivan Pushchin arrived on January 11, 1825. Aleksandr heard the sleigh bells and rushed out of the house in his nightdress. Ivan found him standing barefoot in the snow. Their meeting was joyful. In his diary, Pushchin described the "poetic disorder" of his friend's small room. With its scattered papers and bitten-off ends of quill pens, it looked a great deal like the room he had had at the lycée. Ivan greeted the poet's nanny with a warm hug. He had heard so much about her goodness.

The day passed like one long party. Ivan and Aleksandr talked about poetry and politics. Aleksandr said he was sorry that he couldn't share in his friend's secret activities against the tsar, but he admitted that he could not be trusted because of the "stupid things" he had done. Their happiness was broken only once by a visit from the abbot of the Svyatogorsk Monastery. When Father Jonah entered, Aleksandr put down the play Pushchin had given him and picked up a copy of the *Lives of the Saints.* Father Jonah had the job of reporting to the government on Pushkin's behavior. He was checking to see who Pushkin's visitor was. "When the abbot came in, [Aleksandr] grew quiet like a schoolboy." They were both glad to see the abbot go.

In the third act of Boris Godunov, *Boris calls for his son, and after a moving goodbye, names him heir to the throne of Russia.*

Soon it was time for Ivan to leave. The two friends parted sadly. As Pushchin put it, "We seemed to feel that we were drinking together for the last time and that we would never meet again."

In the middle of April 1825, Aleksandr enjoyed a three-day visit from Anton Delvig. Of his lycée classmates, Anton was now perhaps his closest friend. The two poets had much

Anton Antonovich Delvig, left, *and Ivan Ivanovich Pushchin,* below to talk about. Among other things, they discussed the poetry of Derzhavin, their old favorite from their years at the lycée. Aleksandr now felt that Russian poetry was outgrowing Derzhavin. Aleksandr wrote to Anton in early June: "After you left I reread all Derzhavin's poems, and here is my final opinion. That strange man knew neither the Russian ABC's nor the spirit of the Russian language.... He had no understanding of either style or harmony." He added that a handful of Derzhavin's poems should still be read, "but burn up the rest."

Aleksandr depended on Lev and Anton to send him news of St. Petersburg. He wanted to know if people were buying his books. He had published the first chapter of *Evgeni Onegin*. As it turned out, the critics hated it, but the people loved it. One shop sold 700 copies in two weeks. Aleksandr told himself that the critics didn't matter.

Day by day as the year wore on, he felt a greater desire to leave Russia. He wanted to go to London or Paris, and never return to Russia. He told one friend that he hated his country. He sent Zhukovsky a letter to give to the tsar. The letter stated that he had an aneurysm, a swollen blood vessel, in his leg and needed a foreign specialist to operate on him. The "aneurysm" was only an excuse to escape Russia. All he really had was a varicose vein in one leg. But his friends took him seriously. They began to worry about his health. Zhukovsky kept Pushkin's letter to the tsar and wrote to Nadezhda Pushkin, asking her to write to the tsar. She asked the tsar to send her son to a doctor in southern Russia. The tsar refused. He said that Pushkin could see a doctor in nearby Pskov.

Aleksandr's plan had failed. He wished that Zhukovsky had not written to his mother. Now he wanted to drop the matter, but his friends kept trying to help. He knew that if he

Mikhailovskoye, the Pushkin estate where Aleksandr was exiled

went to a Russian doctor, the doctor would see that he had lied about the aneurysm. Then the tsar would find out that he was trying to escape. Soon Aleksandr was complaining that his friends were helping him so much that he would end up in jail because of all their efforts.

He was going to write to the tsar again, but on December 10, 1825, word reached him that Alexander I had died. Right away, Aleksandr decided to go to St. Petersburg. He thought that with so much important business going on, no one would notice him. When he was riding out to say good-bye to his friends at Trigorskoye, a rabbit crossed his path. Aleksandr was superstitious; the rabbit was an unlucky omen. On his way home, another rabbit crossed his path. He got home only to find that his coachman was sick. Then, when he was finally ready to leave for St. Petersburg and his coach had driven just beyond the gates of his estate, he saw a priest walking along the road. This third unlucky omen was too much for Aleksandr. He decided to stay at home.

It was a good thing. He had planned to be in St. Petersburg on the night of December 13, 1825. The next day an armed rebellion took place in the main square. Many of Pushkin's friends were rebel leaders. Pushkin had planned to go straight to the rooms of his classmate Kondraty Fyodorovich

On December 14, 1925, a group of revolutionaries gathered at Senate Square in St. Petersburg. The revolutionaries, or Decembrists, fired a few shots, but the tsar's cannons ended the revolt.

Aleksandr's drawings of Kyukhelbeker and Ryleyev at Senate Square, right, *and the hanged Decembrists,* below

Ryleyev on the 13th. That night his friends held a secret meeting there. Even if they would not have let Pushkin join them the next day, he would have been accused of being one of them. As it was, the uprising failed. Soldiers loyal to Nicholas I, the new tsar, opened cannon fire on the poorly organized rebel troops—the Decembrists—killing some and scaring away the rest. In the next few weeks, the leaders of the revolt were rounded up and put on trial. Ryleyev and four others were hanged. Many other Decembrists, including Pushchin and Kyukhelbeker, were thrown into prison and then herded off to Siberia.

News traveled so slowly that Aleksandr didn't hear of the revolt until January. By June 1826, it was clear that Tsar Nicholas I believed Pushkin was innocent. The poet wrote to Nicholas asking to be allowed "to go to Moscow or Petersburg or abroad." He also swore that he had never belonged to a secret society and would never join one.

Nicholas I sent a spy to check up on Pushkin. The spy pretended to be a scientist studying plants. He went around the neighborhood quietly asking questions. He spoke with Father Jonah, gossiped with Pushkin's neighbors, and questioned his servants. When he was finished, all he could report was that Pushkin dressed strangely and ate a lot of oranges at the Svyatogorsk fair. Although the poet was kind to his servants, he was not teaching the local peasants to rebel, and he talked very little about politics. This report pleased Nicholas I. In early September, the tsar ordered Pushkin to come see him in Moscow. Pushkin's long wait was over. He was happy — very happy — to go.

Aleksandr at his Boldino estate

⋗ SIX ⋖

The Restless Years
1826-1831

Pushkin met the new tsar in Moscow on September 8, 1826. Nicholas I had just been crowned and Pushkin hoped he would be in a forgiving mood. He was hoping to be granted more freedom. The first thing the tsar asked was whether Pushkin had been involved with the Decembrists. The poet said he would have joined his friends, but luckily he hadn't been able to. Nicholas I liked Pushkin's honesty. Next he asked Pushkin why he didn't publish more poems. Pushkin complained that censorship made it impossible. The tsar then said he would be Pushkin's personal censor. He said he hoped Pushkin wouldn't be foolish anymore; he wished they would not be enemies.

What this meant, of course, was that the tsar expected Pushkin to write poems in praise of him instead of against him. He appointed Count Aleksandr Khristoforovich Benckendorff to be Pushkin's censor. The count would report to the tsar. Every poem was to be sent to Benckendorff before it could be published. Pushkin wasn't allowed to read a poem to his friends without first having the count's approval.

The tsar asked Pushkin to write a paper about Russian education. He thought the poet had learned a lesson about the "bad educational system" that had led to so much trouble for Pushkin and his rebellious friends. Many of the Decembrists had been Pushkin's classmates at Tsarskoye Selo. The tsar hoped that Pushkin would teach the Russian people to be more loyal to their tsar. Pushkin went home to Mikhailovskoye to think. He had two choices: he could write what the tsar wanted him to write or he could write what he himself truly believed. He told a friend that he didn't want to pass up the chance of doing some good. So he wrote a paper in which he said that the best kind of school was one like Tsarskoye Selo, where the teachers spoke freely about politics. Benckendorff wrote to Pushkin that the tsar didn't like the paper. He argued that knowledge was useful only if it helped people to serve the tsar.

Pushkin returned to Moscow. He wanted, first of all, to help his friends who were still prisoners in Siberia. For this purpose, he addressed his poem, *Stanzas,* to Nicholas I. The poem compares Nicholas I to Peter the Great. It says that both tsars believed in spreading new knowledge, and that they both were "firm and tireless" leaders who were also "forgiving." Pushkin was trying to say that Nicholas I should forgive the Decembrists. The tsar didn't listen. But worse than that, the people who read *Stanzas* in the papers thought Pushkin had given in to the tsar. They thought that he had become the tsar's poet and had given up on the people.

They didn't know that he was also writing poems against the tsar. Aleksandr knew he couldn't publish these poems, so he kept them to himself. When he first arrived in Moscow, people had flocked to see him. They had followed him in the streets. Here was the great poet who had refused to obey the

К ***

Я помню чудное мгновенье,
Передо мной явилась ты,
Какъ мимолетное видѣнье,
Какъ геній чистой красоты.

Въ томленьи грусти безнадежной,
Въ тревогахъ шумной суеты,
Звучалъ мнѣ долго голосъ нѣжный
И снились милые черты.

Шли годы, бурь порывъ мятежный
Разсѣялъ прежніе мечты,
И я забылъ твой голосъ нѣжный,
Твои небесные черты.

Въ глуши во мракѣ заточенья
Тянулись тихо дни мои
Безъ божества, безъ вдохновенья,
Безъ слезъ, безъ жизни, безъ любви.

This poem in Aleksandr's handwriting is addressed to a mysterious "K." It begins, "I remember the wonderful moment when you appeared in front of me. . . ."

tsar. Here was a man who wrote about freedom and wasn't afraid to suffer for it. But now the hero had fallen. He was quickly becoming less popular.

Pushkin stayed in Moscow until May 1827. Mikhail Petrovich Pogodin, a historian and novel writer, offered him a job with his paper, the *Moscow Messenger.* He paid him an advance of 15,000 rubles for the year. Pogodin hoped Pushkin would write poems and other pieces that would fit in with the philosophy of the paper. Pogodin and his friends were followers of the German philosopher Georg Wilhelm Friedrich Hegel, who focused on the importance of understanding history in order to understand the present. Pushkin, on the other hand, hoped to be able to change the paper so that it would speak more clearly about Russian problems. As it turned out, he wasn't able to do much at all, because Benckendorff censored his writing.

Pushkin grew tired of Moscow and moved to St. Petersburg in the spring of 1827. By June he was already tired of that city too. The theatres, the clubs, and the parties began to seem stupid and boring. He wrote to his neighbor Praskovia Osipov that he would be moving to Mikhailovskoye and so would soon be seeing her at Trigorskoye. He wanted to go to the country to write some poems that he could sell. He needed money. Lack of money was holding him back from one of his new desires: he wanted to find a wife. Aleksandr was 28 years old. He felt he was no longer young. What good was it to be in the city, seeing so many pretty young women, when he didn't have enough money to afford marriage? Without money, no unmarried lady in high society would take him seriously.

Writing did not go well for him that autumn. He waited to be inspired, but no poems came. So he put aside his poetry

Aleksandr's drawing of himself, 1830

and began to write his first story, a novel based on the life of his great-grandfather, Abram Hannibal.

On his way back to St. Petersburg in October, Aleksandr was reading at the train station, trying to forget about the 1,600 rubles he had just lost playing cards. "I had not read three pages, when four carriages led by an official courier drove into the station." He thought they must be Polish prisoners and went out to have a look. "One of the prisoners stood leaning against a post. A tall, pale, thin young man . . . walked up to me . . . . We stared at one another for a time and — I recognized Kyukhelbeker. We threw ourselves into each other's arms. The guards dragged us apart . . . . Kyukhelbeker fainted. One guard gave him a drink of water, put him in a cart and the troikas set off again. I drove off. At the next station I found out that they were traveling from Schlisselburg. But where to?"

Kyukhelbeker had been sentenced for life to a lonely prison cell. Aleksandr never saw him again. It was impossible to think of Kyukhelbeker as a dangerous rebel. He was a harmless man, even a little bit silly — a follower with few ideas of his own. Aleksandr felt amazingly lucky and yet terribly sad. He had escaped, but many of his dearest friends would die in prison. First they would become thin and pale and hopeless, then they would die. And he was returning to the ballrooms of St. Petersburg.

But the dances still did not make him happy. By the spring of 1828, Aleksandr wrote:

> There is no goal before me;
> My heart is empty, my mind is idle . . . .

In a short period of time he pursued three women. The first was a distant relative, Sophia Fyodorovna Pushkin.

In 1827, Aleksandr started to look for a wife.

Aleksandr wanted to ask her to marry him. In those days, a man proposed to a woman through a friend. Aleksandr wrote to his friend Vasily Petrovich Zubkov to ask for Sophia's hand in marriage. But it was too late. Sophia was already engaged to another man.

Next he turned his attention to Yekaterina Nikolayevna Ushakov. He often visited her mother's house in Moscow between 1826 and 1830. Sophia had been shy, but Yekaterina was outgoing. Once in a letter he had called the two women his "good angel" and his "bad angel." Yekaterina loved to talk with Aleksandr, but had told one of her friends that she would never marry him. This finally became clear to Aleksandr. Meanwhile, he was growing interested in the 19-year-old Anna Alekseyevna Olenin, whose father was president of the Academy of Arts. He was one of the officials who, on June 28, 1828, signed the papers ordering the police

One of the women he wanted to marry was Anna Alekseyevna Olenin.

to watch Pushkin. Aleksandr knew that he had little chance of marrying Anna, but he tried. When he went to see Anna's mother to make his proposal, she said it could never be. She felt, and probably told him, that his position in society was too low, and he was too poor.

When it appeared that Russia was about to declare war on Turkey in April 1828, Pushkin wrote to the tsar saying he wanted to join the army. The tsar refused. Then Pushkin asked to go to Paris for six months. Again he was refused. In October, he visited Praskovia Osipov at her Malinniki estate. Aleksandr could have gone to Mikhailovskoye instead, but his nanny, Arina, had just died and he couldn't bear to be there without her. At Malinniki, Aleksandr finished writing the seventh canto of *Evgeni Onegin* and wrote several other long poems. He spent a happy six weeks in the country, returning to Moscow at the end of November. He was still looking for a wife.

Aleksandr's old friend Vyazemsky wrote to his wife that Aleksandr arrived in Moscow looking sad and then left in early January, still looking sad. The poet had met the 16-year-old Natalya Nikolayevna Goncharov at a party given by his old dancing teacher. He quickly fell in love with her. But he was not very hopeful of marriage. He was worried that Natalya's mother would refuse his proposal for the same reason the Olenins had. When he returned to Moscow in March 1829, he asked for Natalya's hand. Natalya's mother would think about it. This gave him new hope.

In May 1829, Aleksandr left for the Caucasus to visit his brother, Lev, who was stationed there with the army. Aleksandr stayed in the Caucasus for over four months. His brother and Nikolay Raevsky had already gone to the front lines in Turkey. When Aleksandr heard from Raevsky, he moved

*Natalya
Nikolayevna
Goncharov*

south, crossing the river into Turkey. He didn't wait for official permission. He was too excited. It was his first time in a foreign country. On June 13, he joined Lev, Raevsky, and Pushchin's younger brother Mikhail at the army camp. Mikhail Ivanovich Pushchin had been exiled to the Caucasus because of his part in the Decembrist revolt.

Aleksandr drew a sketch of himself with a cossack pike in a skirmish against the Turks.

Pushkin wanted to fight the Turks. On June 19, he had his chance. Just beyond the army camp, the Russian cossacks were fighting the Turkish cavalry. Pushkin rode out with the others to meet the enemy. Mikhail Pushchin and one of his friends saw the poet charging the Turkish line alone. They rushed to overtake him and send him back. The cossacks soon came to their aid and sent the Turks into retreat. For the next few days, Pushkin was angry with the Turks for running away. The Turks continued to move south. He never had another chance to fight them.

Pushkin rode with the Russian army into Erzurum, a Turkish city that had just been captured by the Russians. A group of pashas, Turkish army leaders, met him in the street. One of them found out that he was a poet and greeted him warmly, saying that a poet is equal to the kings of the world. Pushkin returned to the Caucasus on August 1 at the order of General Ivan Fyodorovich Paskevich. The tsar had probably warned the general not to let Pushkin stay in the army any longer with his old friends.

Pushkin kept writing to Pogodin asking for more money. The editor finally sent some. On the way to Moscow in September, Pushkin lost it all gambling. At first, Mikhail Pushchin, who traveled part of the way with him, had made him promise not to gamble. But once Pushkin started gambling he could not stop. He arrived in Moscow only with money he had managed to borrow. Right away he was met with questions from Benckendorff. Why had he left the Caucasus without permission? Why had he crossed into Turkey? Pushkin said he had wanted to see his brother, but this was not a good enough excuse.

Once back in Moscow, Pushkin began to put his energy into Delvig's new journal, *The Literary Gazette.* His enemies, including Benckendorff and Faddey Venediktovich Bulgarin, the editor of a rival journal backed by Benckendorff, wanted to see the *Gazette* fail. They had guessed rightly that Pushkin was the major force behind the journal. Bulgarin attacked Pushkin in his journal, saying that he was old-fashioned, that he was a bad copier of Byron, that he boasted of freedom but was the slave of the tsar, and that he was a gambler and a vain man. In a later essay, Bulgarin stooped to making fun of Pushkin's family. He wrote that Pushkin's great-grandfather Hannibal was bought by a drunken captain for a bottle of rum.

Pushkin fought back, but with a fading sense of purpose. He wrote short, biting poems about Bulgarin's nasty character. But it did no good to attack him. Who was Bulgarin? A nobody. To answer him would be to treat him like someone important. And yet Pushkin's reputation seemed to be at stake. So many people read Bulgarin's journal.

Pushkin's letter to his
censor, Benckendorff, on
March 24, 1830, pleading
for help with his reputation
and an 1830 caricature
of Pushkin, left

Criticism always bothered Pushkin, and insults always stung him. He consoled himself with the thought that he was, after all, a better man than Bulgarin — a better poet from a better family. Bulgarin was full of envy, that was all. Even so, Pushkin wanted to complain to the government. But the only person he could complain to was Benckendorff, and he knew that Benckendorff was the real power behind Bulgarin.

What worried Pushkin even more than Bulgarin's words was the fact that his new poem *Poltava*, about Peter the Great's war against the Swedes, was selling poorly. In one of his notes, he reasoned with himself that young poets will always be more popular because they write of common feelings and experiences. An older poet, on the other hand, who has thought longer and feels more deeply, will be understood by only a handful of fellow poets.

While Pushkin was busy defending himself against Bulgarin, he had other problems to solve. It soon became clear to him that Natalya Goncharov's family had very little money. Natalya's mother had hoped to find a rich husband for her daughter. By the spring of 1830, she had had no luck. Then she turned to Aleksandr. In early April, she agreed to the marriage between Aleksandr and Natalya, but first she made Aleksandr promise to lend her 11,000 rubles for Natalya's dowry. A dowry was a sum of money normally given to the bride by her parents. Natalya's mother also convinced Aleksandr to write to his father asking for one of the Pushkin family estates.

Sergey Pushkin agreed to give his son the small estate of Boldino. Aleksandr mortgaged the serfs and gave the money to Natalya's mother for the dowry. Natalya's mother, who needed the money to pay off her debts, never passed it on to Natalya and never paid Aleksandr back. Natalya's grandfather promised to provide the trousseau — the clothing, bedding, and other items that are the bride's marriage gift from her family. He also borrowed money for the trousseau from Aleksandr and never paid him back.

The death of his uncle Vasily in August 1830 forced Aleksandr to put off his marriage for six weeks. In early September, he went to take possession of the Boldino estate. During his stay at Boldino, a cholera epidemic broke out. To keep the disease from spreading, the police would not let anyone leave. Aleksandr had planned to return to Moscow on September 16, but he had to wait until December 5.

Aleksandr kept trying to leave Boldino. He hated to put off his marriage any longer. But the delay was lucky in one sense. Three months in the empty grey countryside at Boldino gave him time for writing. On December 9, he wrote to his friend the poet Pyotr Aleksandrovich Pletnyov, "I'll tell you a secret: in Boldino I wrote as I have not written for a long time." In all, he wrote one story in verse, the last two cantos of *Evgeni Onegin,* four short dramas that he called the "little tragedies," thirty short poems, and five short stories. He finished the four little tragedies in two weeks. He soon found out that his play *Boris Godunov* — which the tsar had finally approved — was to be published. He planned to publish most of what he had written during his stay at Boldino. He needed all the money he could make.

On February 18, 1831, after much waiting and much emotional pain, Aleksandr Sergeyevich Pushkin married Natalya Nikolayevna Goncharov. The marriage was unhappy from the beginning. On the morning after his wedding night, Aleksandr left the house and did not come back all day. Even before the marriage, he had trouble with Natalya's relatives,

Natalya, left, *and Aleksandr Pushkin, after their marriage*

especially her mother. But afterwards it was worse. Natalya's mother kept telling Natalya that her husband was worthless and that she was too pretty for him. To Aleksandr she hinted that her daughter would seek a divorce. Aleksandr felt that his mother-in-law was ruining his young wife. He wanted to take his wife away from the influence of her mother and to find peace for himself. In June he and Natalya moved to Tsarskoye Selo. Now Aleksandr could ignore his mother-in-law, but he could not ignore the tsar.

Aleksandr walks by the banks of the Neva River in St. Petersburg.

↬ SEVEN ↫

In the Shadows
1831-1837

The year began in sorrow. Anton Delvig died suddenly on January 14. Aleksandr wrote to Pletnyov: "It's sad, agonizing. This is the first death I have ever wept over....Nobody in the world was closer to me than Delvig. Of all my childhood friends he alone was always present to me. He held together our little band of friends. Without him we are like orphans. Count on your fingers how many of us are left: you, I, Baratynsky, and that's all."

Aleksandr's loneliness would only increase with the years. Even so, he enjoyed a moment of peace in the summer of 1831. It was the happiest time of his marriage. In the mornings, he sat at the round table in his upstairs study reading and writing. He sometimes had visitors. His friend Aleksandra Osipovna Rosset would come to hear him read his poems. Zhukovsky and Pletnyov, who lived nearby, would join them for discussions. Some mornings, Aleksandr, Natalya, and Aleksandra drove through the countryside.

Aleksandr would sit on the back of the narrow cart and sing songs making fun of the tsar. In the afternoons, he and Natalya walked together in the park. They lived near the Tsarskoye Selo lycée. Every scene stirred up memories for Aleksandr. He had returned to the home of his youth. Now he was older and sadder, but the peacefulness of the place soothed him.

That soon changed. The tsar and his court arrived on July 10. They had fled to Tsarskoye Selo to escape the cholera epidemic that was then raging in St. Petersburg. Natalya was happy for the change of society. Now she could go to balls and meet people. She often felt left out of Aleksandr's life because she didn't like literature. She was unhappy that she couldn't talk with Aleksandr the way Aleksandra could. Society would give her other things to think about. For Aleksandr, the change was not so happy. His "European beauty," as he called Natalya, quickly became a star of court society. Even the tsar danced with her. By contrast, Aleksandr was cast into the shadows. The rich men of the court cared nothing for poetry. They treated Aleksandr as an outsider because he was poor.

If Aleksandr had been treated better, Natalya's success might have pleased him. But everyone cared for his wife and no one cared for him. The dances led to more expenses. Natalya needed new dresses, the most fashionable ones. Aleksandr was borrowing money right and left. The tsar, who saw Pushkin's troubles and thought that Natalya deserved to be given the best of everything, offered Pushkin a job as an official historian. No real duties were attached to

Aleksandr and Natalya Pushkin arrive at a court ball, where Natalya was the toast of society and Aleksandr was left alone.

the job. He would receive 5,000 rubles per year and would be able to use the government archives for information for his history of Peter the Great. The money wasn't enough, but it helped.

As Natalya's social career was taking off, Aleksandr was leading a more quiet life with his few friends. In early June, he had met Nikolay Vasilyevich Gogol, a young fiction writer. Almost every evening, Gogol, Zhukovsky, and Pushkin got together to talk about writing. Pushkin was delighted by Gogol's funny stories. He said he was surprised to read stories so completely new and fresh. He once scolded Gogol, saying

Aleksandr, right, *and Zhukovsky,* center, *met regularly with the young writer Nikolay Vasilyevich Gogol,* left, *at Tsarskoye Selo.*

it was a crime that Gogol didn't write novels. Then he told the young writer a story that he had meant to put in the form of a poem. Gogol would use Pushkin's story in his greatest novel, *Dead Souls.*

In mid-October, the Pushkins returned to St. Petersburg. The cholera epidemic was dying down and Natalya was wanted for the winter season of dances at court. In the capital, Aleksandr's worries increased. There was always the cost of new dresses, but now his wife also needed a carriage and horses. On top of this, the Pushkins had servant troubles. They had to hire a new cook and replace a few drunken and disorderly house servants.

By October, Natalya knew she was pregnant with their first child. Whenever Aleksandr went out of town, he wrote letters to his wife warning her to take care of herself, not to dance too much, and to get her rest. She did as she pleased and stayed healthy. On May 19, 1832, she gave birth to Maria Aleksandrovna. Aleksandr paced in the halls for hours during Natalya's labor. He was so nervous that he promised himself to go out of town the next time she gave birth.

The Pushkin's second child, Aleksandr Aleksandrovich, was born on July 6, 1833. In August, Aleksandr set out for the town of Orenburg to visit the site of the rebellion of 1773 led by Yemelyan Ivanovich Pugachov. Pugachov had stormed the town of Orenburg, then led his men toward Moscow, raising a peasant army that threatened the power of Catherine the Great—empress from 1762 to 1796. In 1774, the rebellion was finally crushed, due largely to a famine. Aleksandr was writing a history of Pugachov. He traveled from town to town, speaking to the oldest citizens and looking at official records.

On his return trip in October, Aleksandr stopped at Boldino to write. He finished his *History of Pugachov,* as well as his great, long poem, *Bronze Horseman,* and a number of smaller poems and stories. It was another productive autumn. Aleksandr returned to St. Petersburg in November, hoping to publish what he had written and to pay off his debts. The bookseller Aleksandr Filippovich Smirdin planned to publish a journal. He offered Pushkin 15,000 rubles a year to publish all of his new works in the journal. Pushkin needed the money, but first he had to ask Benckendorff if he could publish. He finally got word that the tsar would let him publish the *History of Pugachov* but not the *Bronze Horseman* and several other poems that Smirdin wanted to publish. As a result, Pushkin had to settle for less money from Smirdin.

Seeing that it would be hard to raise money on his own, Pushkin asked the tsar for a loan of 15,000 rubles. Nicholas lent him 20,000 rubles. He also gave Pushkin a new salary and the title of junior gentleman of the bedchamber. This position in the tsar's court was usually given to much younger men who were just starting out in their careers. Pushkin felt insulted. He was angry. He knew that he had been given the position only because the tsar wanted Natalya to stay in St. Petersburg and attend court dances. Pushkin's new appointment gave him no excuse not to attend the balls with his wife. He wanted to go straight to the tsar and refuse the "favor." He would have, but his friends calmed him down and talked him into accepting.

Pushkin accepted, but he clearly despised the tsar from that day on. Aleksandr's diaries are full of complaints and criticisms. At one point he notes that the tsar's holiday celebrations would cost half a million rubles and wonders, "What will the people who are dying of hunger have to say to that?" Although he never openly complained to the tsar, he showed his anger by failing to go to some official ceremonies. He wrote in his diary that he had no desire to parade in a child's uniform with a troop of teenagers. He would rather be whipped in public.

In the winter of 1834, Natalya dragged Aleksandr to every possible dance, and there were many. She was pregnant again, and Aleksandr worried about her health. The dances lasted far into the night. Natalya would return home exhausted only to prepare for another dance the next evening. It finally was too much for her. One night she became sick, and Aleksandr had to rush her home. She lost the baby and almost died herself. On April 15, 1834, Aleksandr sent her to her mother's estate where she could be properly cared for until she felt better.

Meanwhile, Pushkin's enemies were saying that he beat his wife. On the other side, the tsar was ordering him to go to all the official ceremonies. He was supposed to be present at some of the festivities in honor of the tsar's son and heir, the future Alexander II. On April 22, Aleksandr wrote to Natalya that he reported sick and didn't attend the ceremonies, "and now I am afraid to meet the tsar; I shall stay home for this whole round of festivities." He said that he didn't want to bow down to the future tsar whose reign he would probably not live to see.

Pushkin should have known better than to write such a thing in a letter. As often happened, the postmaster opened his letter. When he read what Pushkin had written about the tsar he gave the letter to Benckendorff who passed it on to the tsar. When the tsar read it, he flew into a rage. He thought that Pushkin didn't appreciate his "favor." When Zhukovsky heard about the letter, he told the tsar that Pushkin hadn't meant anything by the letter. The tsar may still have been angry, but he agreed not to punish the poet.

When Pushkin learned that the postmaster had opened his letter, he couldn't contain his anger. It was the ultimate insult. They were robbing him of his privacy. Not even the family was sacred to the stupid officials at the post office. It took Pushkin a long time to get over his rage. He couldn't write with pleasure to his wife. "Please," he wrote to her, "don't ask me for tender love letters. The thought that they are being opened and read by the post, the police and so forth turns me to ice."

Aleksandr's worries were making him ill. He decided it would be best to resign from the tsar's service and move to the country where he could write in peace and save money. On June 25, 1834, he sent Benckendorff his letter of resignation. At the time, Pushkin was settling some business for his father, who was also having money problems. Olga's husband was also hounding Aleksandr for money. On top of this, St. Petersburg was boring him. He needed his freedom. He had to get away.

Benckendorff wrote back to him saying that the tsar agreed to his resignation. However, he said Pushkin would not be allowed to use the archives anymore. The archives, Benckendorff explained, could only be used by men the tsar really trusted. Pushkin understood this answer to be a threat. In other words, the tsar was saying that Pushkin could resign and go to the country if he wanted, but if he did this, he would not be able to continue working on his history of Peter the Great. In addition, if the tsar didn't trust him, he probably wouldn't be allowed to publish anymore. He would have his freedom but no way of earning a living, so he decided not to resign.

A year later, Pushkin again tried to resign. Again he was turned down. He told Benckendorff that he was 60,000 rubles in debt, and half of it was owed to private individuals. The tsar offered him a loan of 10,000 rubles. Pushkin wrote back saying that he needed at least 30,000 rubles. He said that the tsar could hold his salary until the money was paid back. The tsar agreed. At 5,000 rubles per year, it would take Pushkin six years to return the money.

Pushkin's debts were actually twice as much as he claimed. Natalya's expensive taste, added to his own gambling debts and the difficulty of passing Benckendorff's censorship, made it impossible for Pushkin to get out of debt. With the tsar's permission, he began to publish a literary magazine called the *Contemporary*. He hoped it would make him some money, but it didn't.

The Pushkins' second son, Grigory Aleksandrovich, was born in May 1835, and their second daughter, Natalya

Aleksandr and Natalya Pushkin's four children: Grigory, Maria, Natalya, and Aleksandr

Aleksandrovna, a year later. This added to Aleksandr's responsibilities. During his visit to Mikhailovskoye in the autumn of 1835, he hoped to be able to write more poems and stories. But his worries were too great. He wrote to Pletnyov in early October: "I've never had such a fruitless autumn in my life... To be inspired one needs to be at peace spiritually, and I'm not at all at peace."

In March 1836, Aleksandr's mother died. He arranged for her to be buried beside her parents at Mikhailovskoye. He also bought a burial plot for himself next to his mother's. At 35, Aleksandr felt that he was growing old. His face was already wrinkled. His hair was turning grey. When his sister, Olga, saw him in June 1836, he looked thin and was very nervous. He couldn't stand his children's noise. He said to Olga, "If only you knew what a burden life is to me. I hope it will not go on long. I feel it won't."

In fact, his death was near. Georges d'Anthes, the Frenchman who would shoot Pushkin in a duel the following January, had arrived in St. Petersburg in 1834. The Dutch ambassador to Russia, Baron Louis van Heeckeren, had adopted d'Anthes in 1833, making him a very rich young man. Soon afterward, the tsar appointed d'Anthes to the cavalry guards. In the autumn of 1834, Natalya and her children returned to St. Petersburg. D'Anthes met Natalya and fell in love with her. They were the same age. Natalya found it hard to resist the handsome young guardsman. They danced together and were always talking. Soon everyone was talking about them.

Pushkin hated d'Anthes. He would stand at the edge of the dance floor scowling at him. Pushkin's enemies were laughing behind his back. His few friends were worried. Pushkin never laughed any more. He was completely gloomy.

On November 4, 1836, Pushkin received an insulting letter in the mail. He thought that it had been written by van Heeckeren, but it was most likely written by one of van Heeckeren's friends. The letter hinted that Natalya was having an affair with Tsar Nicholas I.

Pushkin immediately challenged d'Anthes to a duel, believing that he also was behind the insulting letter. Van Heeckeren asked Pushkin to wait two weeks. On November 17, d'Anthes proposed marriage to Natalya's older sister, Yekaterina Nikolayevna Goncharov. Aleksandr called off the duel. He believed that d'Anthes was admitting his wrongdoing. Most people were baffled by the proposal because it

Yekaterina Nikolayevna d'Anthes, Aleksandr's sister-in-law, left, *and Georges d'Anthes,* above

was clear that d'Anthes loved Natalya. To everyone's surprise, the marriage took place on January 10, 1837.

Aleksandr did not want to attend the wedding. He never wanted to see d'Anthes or Yekaterina again. However, his friends talked him into attending. They argued that if he didn't, it would only make people talk more; they would think that Pushkin didn't trust his wife. Natalya, in fact, was jealous of her sister. It turned out that she had no reason to be. At the balls following the wedding, d'Anthes continued to pay more attention to Natalya than to his bride. Aleksandr could no longer stand it. He had to act. On January 25, he wrote a nasty letter to van Heeckeren. D'Anthes could no longer keep from dueling with Pushkin. This was what Pushkin wanted. The duel was to take place on January 27. Aleksandr told Natalya he was going to fight d'Anthes. He asked her for whom she would weep. She said, "I'll weep for the one who is killed." Her answer only made Aleksandr angrier.

Konstantin Karlovich Danzas, one of Aleksandr's classmates at the lycée, served as Pushkin's second, or assistant, in the duel. Benckendorff received a message, probably from Danzas, telling him where the duel was to take place so that he could stop it. Benckendorff sent the police to the wrong place, as if by mistake.

The duel took place beyond the Neva River at 5:00 in the afternoon. Thick snow covered the ground. It was very cold and windy. D'Anthes and his second arrived in their sledge at the same time as Pushkin and Danzas. They met behind a line of trees that blocked the view from the road. The weapons would be pistols. The two men were to stand 20 paces apart. They could walk forward five paces to the barriers. Each man could fire one shot at any time. If both missed, they would begin again until someone was hit.

Aleksandr's duel with d'Anthes, just after d'Anthes fired his fatal shot and before Aleksandr fired back

Pushkin was in a hurry to get started. The seconds loaded the guns and marked the barriers. Pushkin reached his barrier first and took aim, but d'Anthes fired first when still a step away from the barrier. Pushkin was hit and fell. "I think my thigh is broken," he said. Danzas rushed to him. D'Anthes was about to approach, but Pushkin called out to him to stop. "I still have enough strength to fire my shot," he shouted. He raised himself a little, took aim and fired. D'Anthes fell. He said he was shot in the chest. Pushkin said "Bravo!" and tossed his pistol into the air.

In fact, d'Anthes had only been grazed in the chest. Pushkin, on the other hand, was seriously wounded. The bullet had deflected off of the top of his thigh bone and had gone into his stomach. On the way home, Pushkin made Danzas promise to tell him if the doctor said he was going to die. He wanted to know. "You cannot scare me," he said, "I

*Aleksandr's
return from
the duel*

do not want to live." On the other hand, he didn't want to let
Natalya know of the seriousness of his wound. As he was
being carried into his house, he told her that no matter what
happened, she was not to be blamed, and she shouldn't blame
herself.

It was soon clear that Aleksandr was going to die. His
pain was great. He had hidden a pistol under his pillow,
which Danzas found and took away. Several close friends,
including Zhukovsky and Vyazemsky, arrived immediately

and stayed until the end. Other people, admirers and complete strangers—the common people—came from all over
Russia to visit the family and express their sorrow. Pushkin
received a letter from the tsar, beginning with the famous
line, "I forgive you." The tsar promised to take care of Pushkin's
family. Yekaterina Karamzin arrived. Aleksandr told Danzas
he wanted her to bless him. She entered the room. He could
hardly speak. She wrote to her son that Aleksandr was very
pale but very beautiful, and "his face expressed complete
calm." He died the next afternoon — January 29, 1837.

Vast crowds stood outside the church where Pushkin's
body lay on January 31. The common people were not allowed to enter for the funeral ceremonies. Only high society

*Aleksandr Turgenev and Pushkin's faithful servant, Nikita
Kozlov, were the only ones sent with Pushkin's body to Svyatogorsk
Monastery to bury it in secrecy, because Benckendorff was concerned
that Pushkin's death would incite a rebellion.*

Aleksandr Pushkin was buried at Svyatogorsk Monastery with only the Osipovs from Trigorskoye, Nikita Kozlov, and Aleksandr Turgenev present.

members had tickets. The church was crammed full. Men argued over who would have the honor of carrying the coffin.

One foreign diplomat remarked: "Only here have we learned for the first time what Pushkin meant to Russia. Before, we used to meet him, we were acquainted with him, but none of you ever told us that he was your national pride." The fact was beginning to take hold with all but Pushkin's most stubborn enemies that Russia had lost its greatest talent. Here was the center of Russia's national literature, Russia's equivalent to England's Shakespeare. Russian readers from generation to generation have continued to find in Aleksandr Pushkin an expression of their own deepest feelings and desires.

"If Pushkin had not existed," wrote the great Russian writer Dostoevsky, "there would have been no talented writers to follow him."

Bibliography

Aitken, Gillon R., trans. *The Complete Prose Tales.* New York: W.W. Norton, 1966.

Arndt, Walter, trans. *Collected Narrative and Lyrical Poetry.* Ann Arbor: Ardis, 1984.

Magarshack, David. *Pushkin: A Biography.* New York: Grove Press, 1967.

Mirsky, D.S. *Pushkin.* New York: E.P. Dutton & Co., 1963.

Nabokov, Vladimir, trans. *Eugene Onegin: A Novel in Verse.* New York: Bollingen Foundation, 1964.

Shaw, J. Thomas, trans. *The Letters of Alexander Pushkin.* Bloomington: Indiana University Press, 1963.

Troyat, Henri. *Pushkin.* New York: Minerva Press, 1975.

Vickery, Walter N. *Pushkin: Death of a Poet.* Bloomington: Indiana University Press, 1968.

——. *Alexander Pushkin.* New York: Twayne Publishing, 1970.

Yarmolinsky, Avrahm, ed. *The Poems, Prose and Plays of Alexander Pushkin.* New York: Modern Library, 1936.

Index

(Numbers in **bold** refer to illustrations.)

Acknowledgments

Special thanks to Peyton Engel at the Pushkin Collection/University of
Wisconsin—Madison as well as P. J. Saine, the photographer, for their help
with this project.

Other illustrations have been reproduced through the courtesy of: pp. 1,
2, Library of Congress; p. 6, Laura Westlund; p. 10, International Picture
Service; pp. 17, 93, The Bettmann Archive; p. 44, The Mansell Collection;
pp. 63, 64, 65, 66, Winnie Klotz/ Metropolitan Opera; p. 77, Bettmann/
Hulton.

Flower of Evil

DEATH-MASK OF BAUDELAIRE

Flower of Evil

A LIFE OF CHARLES BAUDELAIRE

by

EDWIN MORGAN

"He setteth an end to darkness, and searcheth
out all perfection: the stones of darkness, and
the shadow of death."—JOB, XXVIII, 3.

SHEED & WARD

New York · *1943*

MANUFACTURED IN THE UNITED STATES OF AMERICA
BY BURR PRINTING HOUSE, INC., NEW YORK

For
BARBARA *and* HAZEL

Flower of Evil

i

IN 1842, in his twenty-first year, with 75,000 francs, oppor-
tunities for publication almost assured in several of those
new and impertinent journals which were springing up everywhere in Paris, and with a stunning mistress, Baudelaire felt
that life had really begun. He could show his mother that
he could do without her. He could show his step-father that
his talent was not only genuine but something for which
his times were eminently prepared. He was confident that
he could handle the world; that his talent, already perfected,
would bring him the fortune and honor which he considered
his due. He was certain that he could develop himself into
a kind of personal perfection which he had already partially
realized: a hero, assured of his glory, but reserved, indeed,
cold to the uninitiate; in dress, quietly elegant, but decidedly
different; elaborately selective of friends, who, like himself,
were sworn to the cultivation of the beautiful; and, as for
women, to indulge in them, with a cold knowledge of his
doing evil, all the refinements of his passion, so that the
pleasure of the sin would be perfect.

When the break with his family had become decisive, he
took a kind of chill, satanic pleasure in introducing his black
mistress, Jeanne Duval, to his mother. His mother was still
young when Baudelaire's father died in 1827; and Baudelaire's father was in his sixties when he married her. In the
attentions of the ambitious and rising General Aupick, she
found the fulfillment of "the sentiment," as she later
called it, to which she felt entitled as a young woman.

1

Baudelaire did not forgive his mother this second marriage until General Aupick died. He coldly rejected every effort of the General to be friendly or useful. His refusal in 1842 of the considerable weight of his step-father's influence with the Orleans family to find him a place in the diplomatic corps, was the cause of the final break. Madame Aupick had agonized for her son but had clung to her husband; so that it was with perfect manner and reserve that Baudelaire presented Jeanne to Madame Aupick, saying, with the grimacing smile that was later to become so characteristic, "This is my mistress."

Indeed, Baudelaire presented her to all Paris with a flourish. She was not very negroid. His own pen and ink drawings of her show her to be long-eyed, slim-waisted with high breasts and with that rich head of hair that was to play a part in so many of his poems. Théodore de Banville states that she was beautiful, if uncommunicative. One of Courbet's first paintings was a hazy nude study of her. In good weather, Baudelaire would take her in a hired carriage for a drive through the rapidly changing Paris of Louis-Philippe with its streets full of its newly enriched masters, its vestiges of elegant Incroyables and its still unhappy and not entirely subdued masses; or else, with Jeanne in the stunning costumes bought with the first careless inroads into his fortune, he would walk arm-in-arm along the boulevards, stepping into art galleries or peering into the windows of expensive bibelot shops. And if some bourgeois stared or some commoner gaped, Baudelaire would be pleased that he had shocked the enemy and had disturbed the freshly idealized right to arbitrate taste and conduct, which was only then beginning to be named public opinion; for, although Baudelaire, moved by a limited amount of sincere humanitarianism was to go to the barricades for the masses a few years later in 1848, he would not admit to them or to the increasingly powerful middle classes the right to judge art on their own terms or to control the artist's life. In the 1840's, the masses in France, fermented by the new doctrine of socialism, and the burghers, warmed by the infinitely profitable prospects of science, could see nothing beautiful save what might contribute to the realization of Monsieur Proudhon's or Monsieur Auguste Comte's heaven. It was against what Baudelaire considered this gradual strangling of the beautiful, this progress of dullness and uniformity, that he closed himself in the armor of his difference, in his dark clothes, his cold exterior. It was for this reason that, upon entering a café with one of his group, Prarond, for example, he would say in a voice loud enough to be heard above the conversation, yet with his characteristically correct and deliberate articulation, "My dear Prarond, I must tell you that I killed my father this morning"; or else, to some exasperated burgher, "My dear sir, have you ever eaten the brains of dogs? Cooked with a little salt, they are delicious and they have the fine flavor of green walnuts." He said these things deliberately to "shock the burgher"—épater le bourgeois—and to "mystify the imbeciles" not only because, like many of the Romantics, he found this a kind of revenge for what was considered the betrayal of the artists by the bourgeois after 1789, but because he saw behind the pompousness and fatuousness of the bourgeois and in the urge for levelling which they had let loose, a power which threatened "to put out the light of the world," indeed, to destroy him. And it was a pleasure, if only for a moment, to shatter the progress of this inevitability.

Yet, it must be said that he did not intend to use Jeanne as a means of shocking the bourgeois. That was incidental, indeed, accidental. If he wished to punish his mother with the sight of Jeanne, that, too, was another matter. No one knows whether the voyage to the Ile-de-Bourbon, on which his family sent him in 1841 to help him change his attitude toward a selection of a career and toward his step-father, and to shake him free of what his family was certain were disastrous associations in the Latin Quarter, served simply to predispose him to the love of black women. It is known only that he brought back two perfect poems, "L'Albatros" and "A une dame créole," which confirmed him in his resolution to write; that he could not free himself of the vision of Dorothée, a beautiful black girl whom he had seen

Aux pays chauds et bleus où ton Dieu t'a fait naître [1]

and who served as substance of some of his early poems; and that he was hardly settled in Paris before he had taken Jeanne out of a cheap vaudeville and installed her as his mistress.

This was no gesture. When he left his mother's house, he had already in his imagination what he would do and be. Stendhal, Byron, Gautier, Hugo, Pétrus Borel had prepared him for this. He would be aloof from society like Pétrus; he would achieve his victory over the world like Julien Sorel; he would be as bold as Hugo; as free, though not so wordy, as Byron; he would make poetry out of his own soul like Joseph Delorme, with the high artistic conscience of Gautier. At twenty-one, he was already certain that he wanted his particular expression to be uncompromisingly personal and to strike between the eyes by the originality and the unassailable form of its statement. He wished to be surrounded by beauty, to have beautiful furniture and pictures without the necessity of troubling himself about their cost. He wished to have a woman not only perfect in beauty and wise in the vices; but one who, at the same time, would be a shelter. He was looking for something to turn to from the world. He thought he had found this in Jeanne. There was a combination of "child-

---

[1] In the warm and blue lands where your God brought you to light! "A une Malabaraise."

ishness and maturity" in the withdrawn silence in which s...
submitted to his caresses which made him feel close to the
realities. It was with something of a shock that he heard her
first peal of mocking laughter as he read to her the poems
which were so much of himself and a great deal of her. It
was with something of a shock that he returned to his apartment to find her drunk in their "great oak coffin-shaped
bed."

Her caresses were still intoxicating; but in the great eyes
where he had, in the beginning, seen so much, he saw a
coldness, an unresponsiveness "made of steel and diamonds"
that enraged him. He struck her to see if she had emotions,
if she had tears. He became furious at her indifference to
his writing, at her constant whining, her constant niggling
for money. The night he found she had been unfaithful he
beat her till she bled.

And yet he did not leave her. At her worst, he had a conscience about her. When her mother died in the dark recesses
of Paris, he went deeper into his dwindling patrimony to
pay for the funeral. He gave Jeanne every available penny,
let her run up bills in his name. He felt responsible for
what she had been to him "in good faith."

ii

MEANTIME, AT NIGHT he wrote with intensity and speed, for glory and money. In the afternoon, in the correct clothes of a "secretary to the English Embassy," he saw friends and tried to make useful contacts in the literary world, which would advance him to the success he felt inevitable. He worked intensely: his friends Asselineau and Charles Cousin declare that by 1844 they saw the almost completed manuscript of *Les Fleurs du mal*. Furthermore, Jeanne was no longer a great distraction. Baudelaire was disgusted with the flesh. It became inconceivable to him that the act of love with "its violence and grimaces," its "bestial conqueror and its ignoble vanquished," could be anything but sin. This is what, in great part, he was trying to put into his poems.

In the patient construction of these he found a kind of satisfaction, but not the release and calm he really wanted. With Boileau, Racine, Malherbe, Régnier and Gautier for his technical masters, he worked with cold precision, with long and rewarding labor to achieve what he called "the prepared miracle." What he said struck with controlled power. Every line was an entity and each poem was perfect in harmony and dissonance, in what was said and not said. Baudelaire was sure that he was creating something new and great. And yet he was disturbed that the satisfaction ended with the completion of the poem. When it was done, it was no longer part of him. He was disturbed, further, that the miraculous moments of insight, the inexplicable glimpses of truth and the infinite which somehow came at the moment of creation,

6

were only glimpses. He was hungry, like so many Frenchmen, for the Absolute, for the kind of perfection, the sort of peace and love that only God could give. Yet, like so many Frenchmen, knowing this, with centuries of the Church's teaching in him, and destined, like so many of the rest, to turn finally again to the Faith, he allowed himself to suffer the spiritual sickness of his time, looking for an Absolute in the confusion of philosophic, political and economic ideals, in the love of women, in glory, in the perfection of his art. And the perfect spiritual satisfaction which he always hoped to find again in his mother and had not yet found in current thought and other women, he tried to secure also, in spite of the emptiness which seemed to follow every perfect creation, in his poetry. He poured all his power, all his hope for glory into it. And though he was not so much upset any more by Jeanne's lack of response to his work, he was deeply annoyed when, upon sending his mother something he had just written, she would answer simply with a few anxious words about his financial condition and his health.

In contrast to this, at the dinners of the eccentric and periodically rich Créole, Privat d'Anglemont, at the Hôtel Pimodan on the Quay d'Anjou, his readings of his poems, particularly stanzas like this from the dramatic "Vin de l'assassin":

> Elle était encore jolie,
> Quoique bien fatiguée! et moi,
> Je l'aimais trop; voilà pourquoi
> Je lui dis: Sors de cette vie! [1]

[1] She was still pretty,
  Although very tired! and I,
  I loved her too much; that's why
  I said to her: Leave this life!
       "Vin de l'assassin."

would evoke the wild applause of sumptuous models like
Maryxe, whose somewhat smooth nudity had provided Ary
Scheffer his *Mignon,* and Paul Delaroche the central figure
for his *Gloire distribuant les couronnes,* and of unknown but
plodding littérateurs of his acquaintance like Champfleury,
the realist novelist, Le Vavasseur, Prarond and Louis
Ménard, who could not make up his mind whether he was a
scientist, a Greek scholar, a painter or a poet. It was at one
of these dinners that Tisserant, an actor at L'Odéon, in the
exuberance of the moment, commissioned Baudelaire to
write a play around this poem, creating a dominant rôle in
it for him. Baudelaire at once triumphantly wrote his mother
that he was engaged on a grosse machine that would make
him, if not famous, certainly rich; and he began to work
feverishly on this play which Tisserant had neither the authority to order nor the intention to use. While Baudelaire
affected this cénacle a good deal, he was never convinced of
the talent of its members or their judgment. In any case, he
would put his poems quietly away to mature until that time
when he would submit them confidently to a more critical
world.

Meantime, he had found entrée into better literary society
and had made acquaintances who, he felt, would be useful
some day. Already certain that his position in the world of
letters would be at the top, he set out to make contacts with
the leaders of his time. He deliberately cultivated the victorious rebels of 1830, who, while they had lost a good deal
of their color and some of their courage by 1845, were still
the leaders of the Romantics, the core about which a new
French literature was being created. Baudelaire felt that a
polite impertinence was necessary to break into the society
of these important presences. In the street, he deliberately
intercepted Balzac, and by the quick exercise of charm, manner and brilliant talk, worked his way, though not into a

deep friendship with that elegant and harassed man, at least into an acquaintanceship.

While still in school, Baudelaire had sent his first sonnets to Sainte-Beuve, the intimateness of whose *Consolations* had made a considerable impression upon him. Later, on some pressure from Baudelaire, Sainte-Beuve admitted that perhaps his *Consolations* were a kind of *Fleurs du mal* of their time. But these pedestrian, somewhat cold, and superficially emotional poems of Sainte-Beuve do not in the least compare with the profound sincerity, the convincing beauty and the magnificent power of *Les Fleurs du mal*. In any case, Sainte-Beuve wrote a restrained note of acknowledgment of receipt of the poems and thanked Baudelaire for his admiration of Joseph Delorme, which was the pen-name he had used when he wrote poetry away back in his rebel days. Sainte-Beuve was by 1845 what might be called the "official critic" of France. He was intrenched comfortably in his offices at *Le Constitutionnel* where, in his skull-cap and velvet coat, he dictated to his secretary, Troubat, his critical articles for a wide bourgeois audience. Of undeniably great scholarship and gifted with critical powers of exclusively an intellectual order, Sainte-Beuve was rewarded by the life-long and un-shakeable fidelity and admiration of Baudelaire who was enormously the greater poet and by far the more discerning and sensitive critic. Baudelaire, either through the strength of his faith in the character of Sainte-Beuve, or in the hope that this powerfully connected writer might eventually become useful to him, clung to Sainte-Beuve even when it was obvious that the latter wished no part of him. On receipt of Sainte-Beuve's first letter to him, Baudelaire hastened to begin a long correspondence, answered, for the most part, briefly and with a hint of distance; and to supplement his letters with casual and friendly visits to the offices of *Le Constitutionnel*. Sainte-Beuve managed not to be visible most of the time; but when a meeting was inevitable, it is said that he did not relish entirely the effort which Baudelaire made at affectionate intimacy by calling him "Uncle Beuve."

There is something inexplicable, too, in the stiff attitude of severe worship in which Baudelaire held himself before Théophile Gautier. In the drawing-room of the exquisite dilettante, Boissard, at the Hôtel Pimodan on the Quay d'Anjou, Baudelaire made everyone uncomfortable by constantly prefacing every remark he made to Gautier by the word, "master." If there is some explanation of Baudelaire's attitude toward Sainte-Beuve in the statement which he made at a moment when Sainte-Beuve failed him wretchedly, "I love you, dear uncle, more than your work," Baudelaire's attitude toward Gautier might be accounted for by believing that he admired Gautier's work more than the man. In the 1840's, when Baudelaire first met him, the hero of the "Battle of Hernani" was a middle-aged family man, still affecting a beard and long hair and making the most out of his position as head of a literary and artistic group which he dominated by a flamboyant verbosity. The verbosity and kind of good-natured careless usage which Gautier affected, set Baudelaire's teeth on edge; and, if he had dared, however delicately, to correct the spelling of Sainte-Beuve, how much he, a master of terse expression, must have wished to deflate the conversation of Gautier. At that time, Gautier had also achieved something of an official position in the literary world. He was considered an expert on art and did an article regularly for *Le Moniteur*. His conversation consisted largely of gaudy and hastily thrown together comment on pictures; and this must have irritated Baudelaire, who was shortly to turn out an analytically brilliant and incisive form of art criticism superior not only to the criticism of Gautier and Diderot but to any then known to France. Gautier was affable to his disciples and had joined to the free-for-all of his cénacle the stability of the family. Although Baudelaire enjoyed, perhaps at times envied, the cheerful domesticity of the Gautiers, he did not come to admire the father but the writer. He stood always in stiff respect before the author of *Albertus, Mademoiselle de Maupin* and *Emaux et Camées* whose "perfect form" he had begun admiring while yet a student and whose labored emptiness he had quickly outgrown. He seemed constantly to adore Gautier and to be happy to think that, in his climb, he might have so important an influence among his acquaintances.

In his effort to have attachments in the best places, Baudelaire had also sent poems and letters to Hugo. Hugo, "Old Ocean," as Baudelaire called him, was the literary sunshine of Paris in which almost everybody with literary ambitions was trying to bask. Baudelaire was introduced to Hugo by his schoolmate, Ourliac, and by Gérard de Nerval, who committed suicide because, like practically all the writers of France of the time, he had given up God and could not, in his own words, "make reality fit my dream." Hugo's salon, presided over by the gracious Madame Hugo and romped through by the little Hugos, was constantly crowded with admirers, sycophants and literary small-fry. In his robust and democratic manner, Hugo slapped everybody on the back and called him "brother" and "poet." This lack of distinction irritated Baudelaire who at once began to re-examine his youthful opinion of the great man and decided that Hugo, with his violent and uncritical democratic and "progressive" programme and his preposterous affability with the Infinite, was not only a great genius but a great ass. He would turn away from the bellowing of "Old Ocean" to the charm of Madame Hugo, whom he long considered just a little stupid for sharing her husband's opinions, and to the musicales which she arranged and which, while more to Hugo's strident taste than to his own, were at least a relief. He felt that, in any case, by having achieved the freedom of Hugo's salon, he was quickly rising to the position and associations he desired; and it was with great pride that he hastened to relate casually to his mother, at one of their "secret rendez-vous at the Louvre," where he met her in order to avoid seeing his step-father, that he was on great terms of intimacy with Victor Hugo. She, however, seemed unimpressed, and, as usual, timidly anxious and reproachful.

iii

IN SPITE OF THE PERSONAL, particularly financial, difficulties
in which he was becoming gravely involved, he was getting
his name before the public. It did not matter to him then
that in one year he had spent more than half of his patrimony. It was no time to consider when one bought exquisite
and unusual clothes for himself and Jeanne; when one ran
into a rare bibelot or a charming picture for one's apartment; when one sent expensive tea and jelly to the Gautiers
for their hospitality, or had a book magnificently bound at
Lortic's for one's library. Luxury and wealth were to him
incidental, as well as necessary to the artist's life. If he ran
out of ready cash, he would tell the landlord and the shopkeepers to wait: everything would be taken care of in due
time. And there were always people ready to lend money to
such an exquisite gentleman, especially because his step-father
was a General and already in line for even higher honors
from the government. A group of these, headed by a person
named Arondel, was very generous to Baudelaire, particularly since, in those days, there was no limit to the rate and
compounding of interest. Arondel kept an "art" shop on the
ground floor of the Hôtel Pimodan, where Baudelaire moved
after leaving his first apartment on the Ile-Saint-Louis; for
his nomadic life had already begun, the wild scenes with the
landlord on the question of money, the hasty gathering up
of books and papers, the removal to the new apartment, the
leaving behind of the old furniture and the buying of new.
Arondel, who had sold, at fantastic prices, false objects of art

to Baudelaire and had loaned him a great sum of money, was always at the door of his shop, grinning at him as he entered. Baudelaire had further found that he could borrow, at considerable interest, it must be admitted, on sums due him for articles and poems accepted or ordered by publications. But all this did not matter now. These things would be taken care of at the moment of his triumph.

It did not matter, although it was beginning to annoy him a great deal, that Jeanne was attempting to assert a kind of domination over him, was not only intruding in his thinking but interrupting his composition. She had begun to make more constant demands upon him for money, pointing out the sacrifice she was making of her life to him. Just to annoy him, knowing his distaste for dogs, she insisted on having several in the house. She would go into a fury of petulance when, because he was absorbed in his work, he did not answer at once some trivial question. He frequently did not return home at all. At this time, at L'École des Chartes, where he was supplementing his studies interrupted at Louis-le-Grand by an unsubstantiated charge of "friendliness" with a school-mate, he had already met Auguste Poulet-Malassis, the printer who was to become so bound up with Baudelaire's life. He had also met, on one of his frequent visits to the Louvre, Asselineau, a writer with the long blond hair and moustache and fat round face of a good-natured Gallic chieftain, who became Baudelaire's most docile, most devoted and not entirely appreciated friend. Baudelaire frequently and at all hours commandeered the beds or the desks of these men in order to get some sleep and to get on with his work; for now his work was beginning to be remarked.

iv

ARTICLES WERE beginning to be accepted, indeed, requested. He was collaborating on the cynical *Corsaire-Satan* with Champfleury, Mürger, Banville and Auguste Vitu. It was an impertinent sheet dedicated to the dissipation of the pall of ennui which its contributors thought the victory of the middle-classes was placing upon French life. The editor was Lepoittevin de Saint-Alme who, whenever an angry bourgeois would come storming into his office, threatening to beat him for some personal attack, would remove his hat and stand humbly showing his white hair. It accepted one of his first articles, "Choix de maximes consolantes sur l'amour," in which he speaks of the stupidity of woman as being a necessary concomitant to perfect love. It took, too, his somewhat pontifical "Conseils aux jeunes littérateurs," a reminder to young writers that a successful book, article or poem has behind it a great deal of failure. Here, also, Baudelaire tried his hand for the first time at literary criticism. Louis Ménard, a school-mate, and one of his first companions in literary Paris, had, under the name of Louis de Sennenville, written a book of verse entitled *Prométhée enchaîné.* Baudelaire took him to task for resorting to "philosophical poetry, a bastard art." Ménard broke at once with Baudelaire and got his revenge later.

L'Esprit public had also taken an article, "Comment on paie ses dettes quand on a du génie." In this Baudelaire regretted notably that Balzac, among other great French writers, had had to prostitute his genius to money-lenders.

The same publication brought out also his first piece of fiction, *Le Jeune Enchanteur,* a sort of lyrical allegory full of the search for perfection and of the poetic sadness of his time.

To his delight, his novelette, *La Fanfarlo,* in which he elaborated in his principal character, Samuel Cramer, his ideal of the aristocratic aesthete, was accepted by *Le Bulletin de la société des gens de lettres.* It is true that he received an insignificant sum for it, but he was glad to be keeping his name so constantly before the public.

Furthermore, Asselineau and Poulet-Malassis were talking up his poetry everywhere. Arsène Houssaye, editor of *L'Artiste,* had taken "A une Malabaraise," "A une dame créole" and "Don Juan aux enfers," which were announced to be poems from a forthcoming book to be entitled "Les Limbes." In the first two poems, writing with a music and clarity, "as if Boileau and Racine were critics of my form," he gave against a background of tropic tranquility, the picture of the kind of warm "natural," feminine beauty which he preferred.

> Son teint est pâle et chaud; la brune enchanteresse
> A dans le col des airs noblement maniérés;
> Grande et svelte en marchant comme une chasseresse,
> Son sourire est tranquille et ses yeux assurés.[1]

With its striking title, its picture of naked women "twisting under the black firmament" of hell, its portrait of Don Juan calm and still impenitent,

> Tout droit dans son armure, un grand homme de pierre [2]

[1] Her color is pale and warm, the dark enchantress,
Her neck is noble;
Tall and svelte, walking like a huntress,
Her smile is quiet and her eyes assured.
        "A une dame créole."

[2] Erect in his armor, a tall man of stone.
        "Don Juan aux enfers."

"Don Juan aux enfers" gave the public some idea of the difference, the power and the boldness of this new writer. But, on the whole, Baudelaire preferred to hold back his poems for slow reworking, for painful perfecting until he had made a name for which they would be the crown.

v

To HIS ANNOYANCE, because of the interruption to his work, he had been late in 1844 called suddenly home by his mother. When he arrived, he was confronted in the salon by Monsieur Ancelle, Mayor of Neuilly and family notary; by a representative of the Choiseul-Praslin family; by General Aupick and by his mother looking more reproachful and more frightened than ever. It was the family council, hastily called together by General Aupick. Until his death in 1841, the Duc de Choiseul-Praslin, "father of the assassin," as Madame Aupick later called him, had presided at these meetings. It was he who was largely responsible for the Baudelaire fortune. François Baudelaire, Baudelaire's father, had been tutor to the Duke's children and had protected the family during the Terror. At the Restoration, the Duke had seen to it that François was given the agreeable and well-paid position of Secretary to the Senate, and had put in his way other important means of income. François Baudelaire had asked the Duke to assist in administering his estate. Upon François' death in 1827 and the marriage of the Aupicks shortly afterward, the estate was managed by the mutual consultation of this family-council; and equal shares of the income were given to Baudelaire and to a half-brother, Claude, the child of François Baudelaire's first marriage, who had gone to live with his mother's family. In 1842, when Baudelaire demanded his part of the patrimony, this was given to him only tentatively, because, to dispose of any of the securities, he still required his mother's signature.

Upon Baudelaire's appearance before the council, the representative of the Choiseul-Praslins told him bluntly that, in view of the state to which he had reduced his fortune and in view of the amount of debt which he had accumulated, it had been decided that thenceforth the control of the fortune would be placed in the hands of the council; that he would be given a small monthly allowance, part of which would have to be applied to the amortization of his debt already equal to one half of his original fortune; and that he would have to account regularly as to how he proportioned the money to his needs to Monsieur Ancelle, who had been appointed his guardian.

Baudelaire protested. The representative of the Choiseul-Praslins observed that the way in which creditors had been crowding about General Aupick's apartment and office had made the General feel that Baudelaire was not responsible. Stories, too, had come to the General of the black mistress and the expensive clothes. Baudelaire argued that this was nobody's business but his own; and that, with the literary success he was bound to have—was, indeed, already having—he would shortly clear up his affairs. And, taking a glance at Monsieur Ancelle, who sat smiling and nodding in perfect bourgeois equanimity, he shouted that, at his age and in his position—he emphasized the words—he would not tolerate the humiliation of a legal guardian. The representative of the Choiseul-Praslins declared that this was to be regretted but that the thing was already done. Baudelaire turned to his mother and cried that this could not have been done to his pride without her permission; and he slammed the door, saying that he would kill himself.

After brooding over this situation for some time, he, indeed, did stab himself in a restaurant. He was brought to his mother's home. Madame Aupick nursed him. A kind of peace was restored between them. He read his poems to her, and she listened with a vague nervousness. In her turn, she tried to interest him in Joubert, in leading a good, an ordered life; and, as tactfully as she could, she tried to reconcile him with the General.

Madame Aupick was intensely Catholic and pious. She had in her room a large, dark painting of Saint Anthony in the desert, being tempted by the devil and a wicked angel. Baudelaire's father had made a parody of this painting, putting in place of the saint a voluptuous bacchante who held a thyrsus instead of the Cross and who was surrounded by rosy little loves instead of demons. Baudelaire had this painting in his apartment along with a portrait of his father which he kept always in his rooms as a sort of symbol. To Madame Aupick's anxiety about his spiritual life, he replied "with a disdain for humanity" and "a disbelief in everything" which terrified and upset her all the more because she was confident that, "in spite of his extravagances," she, "who had put these qualities in him," was appealing to a person of honor and profound religious faith. Baudelaire coldly crushed these efforts; and to her insistence that she would pray for him, he answered that he could not see how so grand a person as God could be interested in one of so little consequence as he.

And, as for a reconciliation with General Aupick, that, too was impossible. First of all, General Aupick always had in mind the evening when, at dinner with officers of his staff, the young and somewhat bumptious Baudelaire attempted to mystify his guests and ridicule him. For his part, Baudelaire had always in mind the blow which the General struck him the same evening before all the guests. And, even more, as his health was restored, he became more emphatically aware of the impossibility of the situation. While the General lived, he could not have a mother. For love, for so many vague and desirable things, she had become a neces-

sity. It was something he had to lean upon. And
gone. His preoccupation with his poetry and o
his furious love-making with Jeanne and with o
in which he tried to find something which was n
not reconcile him to her loss. The confused and indefinable
"feeling of absence" became unbearable. The sight of his
mother talking with respect and tenderness to the General
made him feel even more bitter and more abandoned. He
suddenly left the Aupicks, returned to Jeanne and more
than ever decided to make a success of his writing.

vi

BUT IT WAS ALMOST impossible to write now, not only because of the thought of his financial situation, but because of actual interruptions. Creditors and bailiffs forced their way in to seize furniture, pictures, books, clothes. Landlords and hotel-keepers even held his manuscripts, locked him out. He found his credit exhausted everywhere, and, in spite of the publication of the poems, articles and stories, the financial return was exceptionally slight. He found, to his great distaste, that he was compelled to go to Neuilly to ask for advances on his income. He had sworn never to go near Ancelle, feeling that with more articles like those which had appeared in *Le Corsaire-Satan,* he could manage until he turned out some money-making novel or play, particularly a play. But the play, *L'Ivrogne,* was still in scenario form and whatever money came from his articles was already accounted for by creditors, absorbed long in advance by all sorts of claims to which he had put his signature. To avoid going to Ancelle, he had even asked for small loans from Gustave Rouland, secretary of the *Société des gens de lettres.* He thought that this swallowing of his pride, this recourse to Ancelle would be only temporary; and, upon his arrival at the modest house in Neuilly, with his customary hauteur, he did not request money from Ancelle, but demanded not only the two hundred francs due, but large advances at once.

But he reckoned without Ancelle. Baudelaire hated him from the moment he knew him to be the symbol of his humiliation. He hated him even more when he saw him surrounded by an atmosphere of bourgeois domestic felicity made up of a dreadful interior of bric-a-brac, a fat smiling wife and a pimply little boy. Baudelaire burst into rage when Ancelle, giving him the two hundred francs due, calmly brushed aside his request for an advance. Baudelaire insisted that this money was necessary to his peace of mind until he could finish an important manuscript on which he was working. Ancelle, with his black notary's suit, his pink face, sideburns already turning gray and bright little friendly eyes, was unmoved. When Ancelle began to snoop into Baudelaire's private life, asking his landlord what women came to his room and how, in general, he was spending his money, Baudelaire raged. He threatened to go out to Neuilly and beat Ancelle "before his wife and son" if he did not stop making innuendoes to Jeanne about her race and "her condition." Baudelaire wrote his mother that this fool, whom she had set on him, was wrecking his life. Indeed, just the day before, Ancelle had thrust in on him when he was talking at a café with Michel Lévy, the publisher, and had forced him to run from the table because, in his bourgeois urge to make himself acquainted with anyone who seemed of importance, he had presented himself to Lévy as "Monsieur Baudelaire's guardian."

vii

IN SPITE OF ALL THIS, he continued to write tenaciously, all night, anywhere he could: at home, when Jeanne slept, possibly drunk; at cafés, or at Asselineau's. And, indeed, he was making a name for himself. In 1845, it occurred to him to write an account of the Salon. To his delight, the editors of *Le Pays* accepted his proposition to do it for them. Equipped with an excellent taste, an eye for composition and color which long hours at the Louvre had given him, and inspired somewhat by his conversations at the Hôtel Pimodan with Boissard, Deroy and Gautier, he added to this a superior critical sense which permitted him to distinguish quickly between what was fraudulent sentiment and what was sincere; what would endure and what would not.

He at once went to the defense of Delacroix, several of whose paintings were being exhibited at the Salon and whose work was still being attacked by the Academies and grossly unappreciated by the current run of critics. Baudelaire pointed out Delacroix's mastery of line and color, and emphasized especially his superbly poetic treatment of his subjects. In polite but restrained terms, Delacroix hastened to thank Baudelaire for speaking of him "as of the great dead"; but Delacroix privately complained to his friends that Baudelaire did not understand him at all and was finding in the paintings too much of his own ideas. Yet, it was Baudelaire who, more than anyone at the time, set the words "genius" and "master" beside Delacroix's name and prophesied with

24

uncanny acuteness that he would stand out in the eternity of art "like a lighthouse."

But Baudelaire did not limit himself to defense. He attacked and enjoyed it. In a Salon, where, but for the paintings of Delacroix and one or two things by Decamps and Haussoullier, he found everything else a desert, he set out to destroy le poncif, that is to say, the technically facile but banal creations which were flooding France; to remove the dead hand of Academism and to harry some of the intrenched names who were the pets of the Academies and the joy of the bourgeois. To this he brought a combination of cogent expression and high wit which enabled him to give a picture of his victim in a few words and, in a few more, to demolish him. To heighten his blows, Baudelaire sustained an austere tone, a reserved style. For the most part, he struck solidly, but without heat. Speaking of Fleury's *Auto-da-Fé,* he remarks, "We note with pleasure some memories of Rubens, capably transformed." Of Granet, he says, "A clumsy fellow full of sentiment"; and with his hatred of the pictures of military life, before which the Parisian badauds were standing in ecstasy, counting buttons and verifying epaulettes, he wrote, "Monsieur Horace Vernet is a soldier who paints." He struck at the profusion of hunting scenes which cluttered every exhibition. "Monsieur Kiorboë," Baudelaire observes, "who knows so well how to decorate the dining-rooms of the nobility, in his 'Wolf Trap,' did not, it seems to me, paint with enough vigor the behind of the dog which is retreating before the wolf."

In his *Salon de 1846,* published as a brochure by Labitte, on the cover of which was announced the imminent appearance of a book of poems by the same author entitled *Les Lesbiennes,* he continued his thrusts, adding to them cogent discussions of the relationship of the public to art. In 1845 he had declared that the bourgeois artist was worse than the bourgeois public; for it was the former, who, by catering to what he thought to be bourgeois desires, depressed the level of taste. The middle classes, he felt, must be invited to encourage a better art because it was to them that all artists were addressing their work. In 1846, he complemented this idea by adding that in no case should art be designed to a democratic taste; for, to him, democracy, whatever else it might be, was fanatically utilitarian, "the enemy of beauty." He cast a cold eye again on "the minutiae" of the School of Ingres which was not as capable as its master of idealizing nature. He took shots at Ary Scheffer for "his ecclecticism which negated everything," and at Monsieur Saint-Jean for his "intolerable pedantry." He made quick recognition of the superiority of Corot and Thédore Rousseau for their harmony, their mastery of light and shadow, their "naturalism moving ceaselessly toward the ideal." In art as in all his preoccupations, he was always seeking the ideal. Further, Baudelaire's discussion of the effect of air on color and of light on values, might well have been one of the sources of influence of Impressionism. His insistence, as against the preoccupation which most artists were then engaged in of putting down with pious detail whatever they saw, that art was "a struggle between the artist and nature," that art was not a business of representing but of "interpreting in a language more simple and more luminous," set him down at once as a critic to be reckoned with.

The press was almost unanimous in praise of this bold young man who, at twenty-five, was so effectively jogging the art world out of its sleep of Academism and was so unerringly putting light on men who were not being understood and on values which were being neglected. In Baudelaire's briefer account, which appeared at this time in *Le Corsaire-Satan,* of the exhibition at the galleries of La Bonne Nouvelle, he thrust aside exhibits of "the young old men of the false school of Romanticism, who can understand nothing of the severe lessons of the Revolutionary School," and went straight to David's *Mort de Marat* as something "cruel as nature"; to the "gripping, strange drama" of Gros' *Le Roi Léar et ses filles;* and to Ingres' *Odalisques* and his portraits of Monsieur Bertin and Madame d'Haussonville, as the only things worth looking at. All this added considerably to his stature. And the newspapers commented generally that Baudelaire-Dufays, a combination of his father's and mother's names which he affected at the time, was a writer "to be watched," a critic who had a mind "logical, proud, distinguished and absolute." Baudelaire was exultant that, while he had made enemies among the small-fry, he had made new and important friends. He was known.

viii

AND IT WAS at this time that he became acquainted with
the work of Poe. Poe's stories and poems at once impressed
him as similar to work he had had in mind to do himself.
(This last has been questioned.) In any case, he did not feel
that the character of a writer of such talent deserved "the
public crucifixion" to which "that mercantile democracy,"
the United States was subjecting it. He was further touched
by the devotion of Maria Clemm to the service of Poe's
reputation and particularly by her unquestioning confidence
in his talent. He even wrote to his mother a letter telling
about the fidelity to Poe of this woman, "who was not even
his mother." Baudelaire felt that the work of so great a man
should not be lost on America but should be known and
appreciated in France. In 1845, in addition to his other projects, he set about the colossal task of translating Poe's work
into French. His first translation, *La Révélation magnétique*
appeared in *La Liberté de penser,* followed by his biographi-
cal and critical sketch of Poe in *La Revue de Paris*. And
although his new friend, Poulet-Malassis, said that he was a
"worse Bohemian than the model" he was defending, and
although most of the critics, to Baudelaire's disgust, insisted
upon spelling Poe's name as "Edgard Poë," the appearance
of the first few of the meticulously and brilliantly translated
stories in *Le Pays* added considerably to the reputation which
the "Salons" had given him. And in the absorption of composition, with his clay pipe or cigar, he worked steadily, intensely, certain of his greatness.

ix

MEANTIME, IN THE dingy houses of the Faubourg Saint-Antoine and in the dark factories of the Faubourg Saint-Denis, the uneasiness which leads to revolution was stirring Paris and, indeed, gradually unsettling all of France. Baudelaire was born into a political and moral confusion and struggle which began when France was torn apart in 1789. From then on, the political struggle had been a story of treason and counter-treason. If France as Republic, Empire and Monarchy could be dominated by identical and sinister opportunists like Fouché and Talleyrand, one did not know where one was politically or whom to trust. The treachery and opportunism of Napoleon's marshals are classic. When Napoleon was foundering, they went over to the Monarchy. For the Hundred Days, they flocked back to Napoleon. After Waterloo, they came back to the Monarchy. It was a group of French officers who informed the Prussians at Waterloo of Napoleon's specific weaknesses. After 1789, the governments, whoever headed them and no matter whether there were efforts made at conciliation or oppression, were all unhappy and nervous. In Baudelaire's time, the ceaseless and complex struggle between Jacobins, Orleanists, Bourbons and Bonapartists was further complicated by the presence of the Socialists. Furthermore, the question of political allegiance was odd and involved. Louis-Philippe tried to be more liberal than the liberals who, for all their talk of democracy, by law limited the French electorate to 100,000 out of 30,000,000. The Protestant Guizot was always playing for

Catholic support. By 1847, the population of France, torn in great part from its agricultural base, was crowding into the cities for work in the factories. Public works and the dole were not sufficient to provide for the surplus of the wretched.

With these political and economic confusions, there was an equally complex and disconcerting war of ideas. The Catholicism, which had been for so long the repose, the solution of so many problems of life and death for France, had been shaken by the Revolution from its authority. In the ensuing efforts to find something to take its place, all sorts of combinations and expressions of conscience and thought sprang up. Baudelaire's father, for example, had worn both the cassock of a lay brother and the red bonnet of the Revolution. With Rousseau, it was believed that the individual, keeping the state in a helpful but subordinate position, would solve all his own problems. This attitude was strengthened by the rise of faith in science: man would, of his own powers, be able, in time, to know and do everything. But the Socialists were already challenging the self-sufficiency of the individual. In the misery which the machine was creating, in the contradictions of scientific conclusions, people began to question the power of science and to perceive definite limitations. Into these searchings and doubts, Freemasonry injected its peculiar sort of hope. Many tried to come to rest in the mysticism of Swedenborg, in the tortuous ramifications of the half-science of Lavater and Gall, in oriental fatalism. People wished to be positive about something, to reach some sort of stability. They shifted about and somehow felt abandoned; and the poets were uneasy.

When the Revolution of 1848 burst under the whip of Odilon Barrot's reformism, the lash of Proudhon's socialistic preaching and the intoxication of Lamartine's windiness, Baudelaire was participating in these intellectual and moral confusions. In his "Salons" of 1845 and 1846, he had clearly indicated that the mob was the enemy of "Raphael and roses," of Watteau and beauty. In his first discussions of Poe, he had declared that he could not bear to be ruled by "100,000,000 kings." In his elaboration of the cult of the dandy, he had declared himself definitely the aristocrat, not by blood, but by attitude; the enemy of everything the mob stood for in art and in life. In his conversation and writing, he had ceaselessly observed how much the "enormous imbecility" of the multitude disturbed him and how uneasy he felt under the eternal "smile of Voltaire," which he seemed to see in the eyes and on the lips of almost every Frenchman.

Yet, we find him in 1846 and 1847 constantly in the garret of Pierre Dupont, whose republican and socialistic poems he praised enthusiastically. We find him, perhaps under the influence of the austere Leconte de Lisle or of his more politically-minded friend, Hippolyte Castille, or following the literary examples of Dumas père, Bouilhet and Balzac, who ran for deputies, electioneering and agitating in cafés with Poulet-Malassis and Asselineau. We find him somehow prowling about the back streets and plotting with Proudhon himself. We find him, indeed, founding with Champfleury and Toubin, with the artistic collaboration of Courbet, a revolutionary newspaper, *Le Salut public,* which they edited on the tables of the Café de la Rotonde two days after the precipitous flight of Louis-Philippe, and which collapsed after two editions because the newsboys omitted to bring back the money. And finally, we find him actually under fire at the barricades during the events of June 23 to 26, when over ten thousand were shot down. Then, disgusted with the action of the masses, who, after being given universal manhood suffrage through the eloquence of Lamartine, proceeded at once to elect Louis Napoleon as President

of the Second Republic, he declared himself through with
politics forever.

His conduct during the Revolution may be explained in
various ways. It may have been, as he observed later somewhat fatuously in *Mon Cœur mis à nu,* that the true artist can
play any side of a question with equal power and equanimity. It may have been that, under the influence of the Bousin-
gots, particularly under that of Pétrus Borel, he developed
a hatred of the middle classes for their betrayal not only of
the political and social purpose of the first Revolution but
of the intellectual and artistic programme as well. The artists,
the thinkers and the masses had been used to perpetrate a
strictly middle class triumph which had been emphasized,
in the reaction, by the way in which the bourgeois had politically limited the masses and had attempted to dictate the
morality of art. In reprisal, artists and writers had been constantly attacking and caricaturing the bourgeois. On the stage
and in his drawings, Henri Monnier had, in his creation of
"Joseph Prudhomme," held up to ridicule the intelligence of
the middle classes. In the figure of "Robert Macaire,"
Daumier had been relentlessly attacking the political bourgeois. Renan had been striking constantly at what he called
"the intrenchment of the Scythians"; and, in *Bouvard et Pécu-
chet,* Flaubert had made his attack upon bourgeois thought
and morality. At this time, to be an artist of any sort of consequence, implied hatred of the middle classes; and Baudelaire, while he was convinced that the financial success of the
artist was bound up with and dependent upon the attitude
of the middle classes, had always attacked and abused them.

It may have been that this popular outburst gave him an
opportunity to get even with his step-father. As a school-
boy in Lyon in 1833, Baudelaire knew that it was his step-
father who had crushed the strike of the silk-workers led
by Pagès, burning their homes in Le Gourguillon and riding

them down without mercy. He knew that it had been this business which moved the General ahead so rapidly in the army. It may have been this knowledge added to a feeling of resentment that this sort of man had taken his own place in his mother's preference that urged him to work for the masses. It is said that at the height of the fury of the fighting at the barricades, Baudelaire, waving a rifle, tried to organize a mob, screaming, "Let us go and shoot General Aupick!"

x

In any case, while the election and the subsequent coronation of the second Napoleon took him from then on entirely out of politics, he did not renounce participation in the war of ideas which continued under the Second Republic and the Second Empire. He could not bear the spread of popular journalism, these papers which "with their daily freight of perfidy and crime, one cannot touch without nausea." He was sickened at the rapid and unprecedented spread of industrialism, of Monsieur Guizot's railroads with their accompaniment of frightful bill-boards. He felt that while, as an artist, he must accommodate himself to these changes, he could not admire them. More than anything else, he could not stomach the fury with which, in spite of "the order" and censorship which Louis Napoleon enforced, the ideas of democratic levelling and the campaign against religion were pressed. He found himself "contending in cafés, drawing-rooms, everywhere," against Saint-Simonism; against "that frightful Saint Marc-Girardin" who was preaching, "Let us be mediocre"; against the inspired project, led by Hugo, to bring all values within the reach and comprehension of the crowd. Baudelaire argued that the crowd had to be whipped politically for its own good; that man was not infinitely perfectible and certainly not of that primitive goodness of which the Romantics were so completely convinced.

Trying to untangle himself from the "scientific" findings of Lavater and Gall, he insisted that no one is responsible for man but himself; that there was no other explanation of man's chronic sinfulness than that he was born in sin and could only extricate himself from it by the exercise of his own will. Under the influence of Joseph de Maistre, "that warrior of the Holy Spirit," whose *Nuits de Saint Petersbourg* was shaking the Gallican Church and re-asserting universal papal authority, Baudelaire declared irreligion to be simply "canaille," a destructive force set loose by the growing "enemies of the sublime."

While these feelings did not stir him at once to any personal religious action, they served to move him further from general contact with the world, to make him more dependent upon his own thoughts, to redefine to a great extent certain religious principles as much a part of him as his blood, and to make him more intense with his own preoccupations. He resumed his cold exterior. He declared himself concerned exclusively from then on with the success of his own work. He gave himself up with almost monkish austerity to his writing. He saw very few people. His room became cell-like. Courbet, who painted him at this time, and who complained that Baudelaire's face was never twice the same, shows him pale, with close-cropped hair, bending assiduously over his manuscript. He is quite changed from the youthful portrait by Deroy. The long hair, the little beard are gone, as well as the sweep of a complicated, though reserved, elegance. Baudelaire's dandysme is even colder now; his elegance, as recherché but more subdued. He was re-enforcing his exterior against the world in order to achieve, with the least outside interruption, the perfection of the beauty which he felt he held within him and which he must express with the minimum of delay so as to enjoy as quickly as possible the rewards of its consummation.

For financial reasons, there was a brief interlude of journalism, first in Paris in another quickly disastrous venture with Champfleury, then at Châteauroux, where, it is said,

Arthur Ponroy offered Baudelaire the editorship of *Le Jour-*
nal de l'Indre, a somewhat liberal, indeed, socialistic organ
owned by bourgeois stockholders. At the dinner at which
he was to be presented to the stockholders, Baudelaire, who
was at that time temporarily separated from Jeanne, arrived
with a common little trollop whom he introduced as Madame
Baudelaire. During the meal and the conversation which
followed, Baudelaire sat coldly silent. When asked why he
did not participate, he is said to have replied, "I have nothing to say. Have I not come as the servant of your intelligence?" When one of the stockholders upbraided him for
trying to pass off the girl as his wife, saying, "Monsieur,
that is not your wife, that is your mistress," Baudelaire is
supposed to have answered with his chill politeness and his
slightly grimaced smile, "Sir, the mistress of a poet sometimes may be as good as the wife of a notary." His connection with this paper is said to have been very brief.

xi

IN ANY CASE, back in Paris, feeling more bitter because his mother had gone off to Constantinople with "that man"—who had been named Ambassador to Turkey—and back with Jeanne, Baudelaire sank himself in his translation of Poe, for which he had found a publisher in Michel Lévy; in the preparation of his play and new articles; and in the slow polishing of his poems. But the sums he received from his two "Salons," from the occasional articles and the first translations of Poe having made only a slight impression on the mounting interest, his creditors gave him even less peace than Jeanne. And he suddenly appeared with his black mistress in Dijon before the startled keeper of a hotel, asking with elaborate coldness for a "large room to walk in and a large table to write on."

But Dijon, for all the surcease it gave him from his creditors and for all the opportunity it offered for comparatively quiet writing, was too far from Paris, "that branch-office of hell," the background and the associations of which he found more and more necessary for his work and his advancement. In Dijon there was no one to talk to but Jeanne; and, furthermore, Neuilly was too far away for him to send even Jeanne for those necessary and constant advances on his monthly allowance. And so, as soon as Ancelle, with considerable personal assistance from Madame Aupick, could ransom him and his belongings from his hotel-keeper, he returned to Paris.

xii

BETWEEN THOSE ENDLESS trips from Paris to Neuilly to be
cross-examined by Ancelle; in intervals between hiding from
creditors and scenes with landlords; between nagging letters
from his mother in Constantinople where news of his mounting financial difficulties kept coming; between endless dis-
putes with Jeanne, Baudelaire continued to make new literary acquaintances of importance and, in spite of involving
himself in all sorts of fantastic and get-rich-quick literary
projects, to make progress in the kind of writing he wished
to do.

He had made, indeed, a valuable new friend in Flaubert
to whom he had sent poems and letters. Flaubert had answered kindly and had even invited him to his retreat at
Croisset. He had made another good friend in Théodore de
Banville, whose charming, innocuous verses Baudelaire respected rather than admired. At Banville's home, Baudelaire
enjoyed—indeed, it might be suspected, envied—the pleasant
good taste and serenity of the interior, the quiet friendliness
of Madame de Banville, the poet's mother, who had always
been confident of her son's genius. Banville's quick success
with *Les Caryatides* had left him entirely unspoiled.

In Barbey d'Aurevilly, Baudelaire found also a devoted
friend, but one who did not make him feel so much at ease
as Flaubert and Banville. Barbey's books had already been
written; his reputation had already been made. He was, when
Baudelaire met him, something of a legend. His books, *La
Vieille Maîtresse, Le Dandysme, L'Amour impossible,* written with a studied impertinence and without too much profundity, had set him down as a satanic, a Byronic, a follower

of Maturin, something of a Mephisto who was a devil with women and "liked to eat his lamb raw." He was something of a middle-aged devil when Baudelaire first visited him at his apartment in the Rue de Vaugirard which he had fitted up like the inside of a church, and was busy running around with an Englishwoman of no great beauty, getting his picture taken in the costume of Mephistopheles, wondering whether it was time for him to get back into the Church, and getting out a rather irresponsibly written column on books for *Le Pays*. Barbey was flattered that Baudelaire called him "wicked old man," and sent him copies of his poems. He recognized in the poems which Baudelaire showed him "the impiety" which had characterized his "own youthful work"; and was confident that Baudelaire was a writer "of force," "a thinker, who," as he wrote to his friend Trébutien, "has our hatreds but not our faith." While Baudelaire was flattered that he had got the attention, and, perhaps, the critical support of so well-known a literary personality, he was upset that Barbey saw only "the impiety" of his work. Indeed, he began to wonder uneasily about the penetration of Barbey's judgment when he wrote on the occasion of the appearance of one of Baudelaire's translations of Poe that "Poe was the king of Bohemians and Baudelaire has translated him twice: in his work and in his life." Baudelaire wrote to Barbey at once, reminding him gently and amicably that neither Poe nor he was a Bohemian; that he must not take appearances for fact. Barbey apologized flamboyantly. But Baudelaire was troubled that a man placed so high and so responsibly in literary criticism did not trouble to look below the surface. If Barbey could do this, what about others who did not have even Barbey's perception or power of appreciation? He began to see the necessity, when his poems should be ready for publication, of not just circulating his book generally to the press, but of choosing his critics carefully.

xiii

MEANTIME, THE PRESSURE of financial necessity made him try to get out any sort of work which would bring him money quickly. He had in mind always Poulet-Malassis' suggestion that almost any kind of novel would bring in immediately from "a thousand to two thousand francs." He listed a series of titles for stories which would be positive money-makers: "The Teachings of a Monster," "The Virgin Mistress," "The Idiot's Mistress." He spoke to Ancelle of a novel which, he was certain *La Revue des Deux-Mondes* would surely order; of a play by Diderot which he was going to arrange for Hostein, manager of Le Théâtre de la Gaîté; of several plays of his own, which he "had upon the stocks," namely "L'Ivrogne" for Tisserant at L'Odéon and "Le Marquis du Premier Housards"; of "a big proposition" for a new magazine, involving "some twenty thousand francs."

Although he had determined to keep this sort of work subordinate to his principal projects, he had made up his mind to be a literary factory like Dumas; a Hugo who could write twelve hours a day, standing at his desk; a Balzac who worked feverishly against time for money. But he did not have the strength of these men. Furthermore, he did not have the facility. As a matter of fact, he despised facility and struck at "le style coulant" every time that he found it in his contemporaries. He was an intense writer. Every word must do exactly what he wished. He would work over words for days, weeks, looking not only through French and English dictionaries but, as Léon Cladel reports, through Latin,

Greek and even Hebrew dictionaries as well. At this time, even when he needed to drive himself hard for quick results, he would sometimes, because of a single phrase, hold up a manuscript for long periods and radically upset for months the plans of editors and of publishers. He fussed with the pretty little piece he got out at this time, "La Morale du Joujou," which *Le Monde littéraire* had taken; and with *L'Essence du rire* in which he decided that laughter was not of God, that it sprang only from imperfection—he would rush into the offices to change, strike out, call back and re-read his manuscript, so that nothing imperfect should come from him.

He was particularly upset and tried by the work he was then doing on his translation of Poe. He had learned English from his mother, who had been born in London and who had spent a good part of her girlhood there; but neither what he knew from her, nor what the dictionaries said, satisfied him. He would go to a bar where there was an English bartender, or intercept stray Englishmen and Americans any-where, and discuss with them meanings and special render-ings of words. And, even when his first group of transla-tions, *Histoires extraordinaires,* was completed and was being printed in book form by Michel Lévy at the same time as they appeared serially in *Le Pays,* he still found plenty of changes to make. He dreaded that in the book some gross errors might be perpetrated. And there were plenty of errors com-ing in on the proof-sheets from the printery at Corbeil. In winter, insufficiently clad, he would run down to Corbeil, take charge of the job himself, and effect so many changes that new forms had to be made. There were scenes with Michel Lévy.

Ill health now began to trouble Baudelaire. From irregular and bad eating, he began to suffer from his stomach. As a quick remedy, he took laudanum. Asselineau reports that often, without having had breakfast, Baudelaire would order only dessert at lunch time because he had "neither time nor money for anything else." He began at this time to suffer also from sleeplessness and to have those dreadful dreams in which Mariette—the nurse who, upon the marriage of the Aupicks, took care of him from his seventh to his tenth year when she died—seemed to be always sitting in a corner of his room, watching him.

xiv

IT WAS WITH RELIEF that Baudelaire welcomed his mother back to Paris. He had now someone to confide in, to take his plans, his anxieties to; one who, in spite of her marriage to Aupick, could give him some of the feeling and understanding he desired. He was always seeking the security of a sure and unshakeable love and peace. She had returned from Constantinople on her way to Madrid, to which city her husband had been transferred as Ambassador. She was staying at the Hôtel du Danube where Baudelaire did not visit, of course, because he did not wish to meet General Aupick; but he received her with affection, indeed, effusion at his own rooms, ordered for her elaborate dinners which he could ill afford, at La Tour d'Argent; took her for quiet walks at Versailles and Saint-Cloud. So acutely anxious was he for a satisfying affection that he seemed to forget the long exchange of somewhat acrimonious letters he had had with her while she was at Constantinople, in which he begged, indeed demanded, money and blamed his financial impasses with Ancelle on her misguided maternal instincts, and in which she upbraided him for his improvidence and pleaded with him to make another effort to get order into his life. He seemed to revel in her company, making constant demands for frequent visits during her short stay. And, even when she would renew her timid reproaches and the plea he used to hate so much that he "should try to be like other people," he did not get angry. When she left for Madrid, they were on better terms than they had been for a long time.

At this time, also, Baudelaire felt that it was better to leave

Jeanne. What with his creditors popping at him from all sorts of places, from his closets and even once from his cabinet de toilette, he could no longer bear the tantrums of Jeanne and get on with his work. He began to feel a greater need for peace, a peace not of the world he was beginning to despise. He was suffering from a spiritual malaise, an emotional emptiness, a doubt of the complex society he was in, because he was seeking the Absolute which, like his contemporaries, he had abandoned, but was always seeking—in everything except the Church. But he could think only of getting away from Paris. At one time, he had determined to go back to L'Ile-de-Bourbon where he had had a glimpse of what seemed perfect tranquility and where, indeed, the Creole planter with whom he had visited on his voyage and for whose wife he had written one of his first poems, "A une dame créole," offered him a place as tutor to the children. The thought of taking ship, of getting away, of finding repose in the lush warmth of the tropics, held him often, got into the substance of his poems, compelled his imagination between the harrying of his creditors, his struggle to work, and the daily violences with Jeanne. But he thought that it would not be wise to leave Paris, now that he had made so much progress. In any case, he felt that, for his own efficiency and peace of mind, he must somehow leave Jeanne.

The thing was not easy to do. In the first place, Jeanne had suddenly aged considerably, "shrivelled," as he put it, and had become ill. And even though her illness increased the acrimony of her attacks, it was a matter of honor not to leave her in this condition. Furthermore so many years of propinquity had made of Jeanne a sort of habit. She had been, as he said, for so long his only friend and his "only distraction." He felt under obligation to her also because to the government pawn-shop, which was one of Louis Napoleon's contributions to the welfare of the people, she had carried all her finery. Moreover, he hesitated to leave her "after what she had been" for him. He meant that, after all, it was she who had inspired the substance of many of the poems which gave him the most satisfaction, even though she did not understand or care for them. For so many years she had been his mistress; and he felt an eternal obligation to her for this, even though he had never found in the kind of love at which she was so perfect, the solutions, the peace which he thought must be in it even when he had surrounded it deliberately with enhancements of the senses and had brought to it the stimulus of a willing imagination.

He felt that a change in his attitude toward love might clarify his literary purpose, help him to come more quickly to repose. The incurable hunger, the sharp sense of absence, was always upon him. And again, though the thought of God pressed upon his feelings and his intelligence, even was now beginning to shine through his poems and to be intimated in other writings, he still looked, hopefully, though not with as much confidence as before, to the world to assuage him. He had a remembrance of a moment with his mother—as a child, before his father's death, laying his head in her lap in a carriage, amid her silks, furs and perfume, he had become aware of an enormous sense of well-being, an animal and spiritual contentment which, with the unexpected marriage of his mother, he was never to experience again. It was a kind of deliverance for which he seemed always to be searching. He had sought it in the perfect body of Jeanne. Perversely he had sought it, with a deliberate effort at degradation of his desire, in the imperfections of Louchette, "the horrid Jewess." What he wanted was shelter, "to sleep in the shade of the breast of the giantess," "like a village in the shadow of the mountain." He was looking for the perfection and the peace of the Absolute in women as in art. An exclusively physical love began to sicken him.

What he sought in love simply was not there. He could not bear to be defrauded spiritually any more. And, with the added reason that he "did not wish his friends who had known Jeanne in her beauty to have the satisfaction of seeing her in her decay and distress," he left her, promising to look after her needs even before his own. Jeanne, however, came often to his hotel room to demand money and to berate him for not giving her more.

Meantime, Baudelaire thought he had found in two women that holiness and comfort, that quality of "madonna and mistress," of "sister and mother," which he had been look-ing for in the faces of so many women, even when he was living with Jeanne. The first was Marie X, a model. He saw her for the first time posing at a friend's studio; then at' Henri Monnier's salon. But she at once rejected his circuitous and somewhat literary advances. Abashed by her prompt refusal, he wrote her that it was indeed better that way; that, being beyond the degradation of his touch, she would always remain a symbol of purity, a resplendent and impossible goal. She did not answer or in any way encourage Baude-laire's correspondence and he turned his attention entirely to Madame Sabatier.

Madame Sabatier was already the mistress of Hippolyte Mosselmann, the dilettante son of a rich Jewish banker. Her somewhat plump beauty had been the subject of Clésinger's bust, *La Femme piquée par le serpent,* of Ricard's *Femme au chien,* of sketches by Meissonnier and of a painting at-tributed to Barye. She was vivacious; and her sparkling, though somewhat highly colored, wit dominated and enter-tained a group of artists and writers who thronged her salon in the Rue Frochot and ate her elaborate suppers, the ex-penses of which were paid by Monsieur Mosselmann. Gau-tier, Clésinger, Courbet, Du Camp, Feydeau, the Goncourts, Meissonnier and Rouvière, the actor, were frequently present at these gatherings over which she presided. She was called by Gautier, with classical affectation, Algaë, and by others, with a good deal less respect, "la vivandière des artistes." In any case, whether he was impressed with her vivacity in contrast with Jeanne's taciturnity and surliness, or overwhelmed with her pink and blond health and freshness, Baudelaire quickly made her his idol. Only this time, he decided that he would keep his distance; would keep his feelings, if not secret, at least anonymous.

Over a period of some five years, he sent her, without his signature, a series of exquisitely finished poems which piqued Madame Sabatier's curiosity enormously and both disturbed her delightfully and flattered her. The first of them, "Tout entière," asking

> Parmi toutes les belles choses
> Dont est fait son enchantement,
> Parmi les objets noirs ou roses
> Qui composent son corps charmant,
> Quel est le plus doux. . . .[1]

celebrated "the black and pink" harmony of her beauty which he declared beyond analysis. The second and third, the magnificent sonnet beginning,

> Que diras-tu ce soir, pauvre âme solitaire,
> Que diras-tu, mon coeur, coeur autrefois flétri,
> A la très belle, à la très bonne, à la très chère
> Dont le regard divin t'a soudain refleuri? [2]

[1] Among all the lovely things
Which make her lovely
Among the blacks and pinks
That make her charming
Which is the loveliest. . . .
"Tout entière."

[2] What will you say tonight, poor solitary soul,
What will you say, my heart, once blighted,
To the most fair, the most good, and the most dear,
Whose sudden glance has brought you back to flower?
"Que diras-tu ce soir."

and "Le Flambeau vivant," which spoke of her as

Me sauvant de tout piège et de tout péché grave [1]

admitted the elevating influence she had upon him, "that sweet authority" which required that he devote himself only to the creation of the beautiful. But in the fourth, "A celle qui est trop gaie," Baudelaire, naturally sombre and already a prey to so many vicissitudes, by a kind of lover's perversity declared that he wished to destroy the health that sprang "like light from her arms and shoulders," wished to wound her "astonished" beauty, and to silence her laughter. And in "Reversibilité," he asked,

Ange plein de gaîté, connaissez-vous l'angoisse,
La honte, les remords, les sanglots, les ennuis
Et les vagues terreurs de ces affreuses nuits
Qui compriment le coeur comme un papier qu'on froisse?
Ange plein de gaîté, connaissez-vous l'angoisse? [2]

and declared that, while many might ask for the freshness of her beauty, from "an angel full of so much happiness" and good will, he asked only prayers.

At this time, 1853, he felt somewhat further uplifted, somewhat further secured to some sort of base, by the return from Madrid of his mother, this time for good. While Baudelaire was hurt because he had to learn the exact time of her arrival from a third party, he was delighted to have her back. General Aupick had been retired from the diplomatic service, and the government had made him a Grand

---

[1] Saving me from every temptation and from every heavy sin.
  "Le Flambeau Vivant."
Angel full of gayety, do you know anguish
Shame, remorse, sobs, ennui
And the vague terror of these frightful nights
Which crush the heart like paper crumpled?
Angel full of gayety, do you know anguish?
  "Reversibilité."

Commander of the Legion of Honor and a Senator of the Empire. Baudelaire declared that this was the sort of honors fit for a man like Aupick. He avoided his step-father with the same intensity, but hastened to make arrangements to see his mother as frequently as possible. Baudelaire declined absolutely to frequent her Mondays in her new apartment, because he said that not only did he not wish to meet the General but he could not bear the sight of the Aupicks' friends. He insisted upon their resuming their rendezvous at the Louvre, their walks in the gardens at Versailles and at Saint-Cloud. And, while there were moments of almost complete affection and understanding between them, they could not keep down their differences, which turned constantly on the question of glory in literature and on the question of money. She would listen in a kind of submissive but unconvinced and solicitous silence to his talk about the solid progress he was making with his work and about the financial independence which, he told her, he would certainly achieve.

He would turn on her in a rage because she would hesitate to advance further money to him. All during her stay at Constantinople and Madrid, she had been sending little sums to bolster his small allowance and meagre income against which his appalling debt was mounting. He would reproach her for her caution in giving him a small sum when he badly needed a larger one; reproach her for her lack of faith in his talent, which made her withhold that small extra amount necessary to bring him for the moment required peace of mind and to help him release his energies for his work. He would insist that the sum for which he was asking was, after all, a loan which would take him out of a momentary but desperate difficulty. She would refuse always with the reproaches and the little homilies which he so much detested. She would refuse with the feeling that her refusal would induce him to be more self-reliant, more responsible. He would rage. She would leave him; and reaching home, in a torment of worry, would send him more than the amount he had asked. He would answer in an effusion of gratitude.

In his intense preoccupation with his work, in the increasing demands which his creditors were making upon every penny of his allowance and every sou of his small income from his writing, he found himself, more than he liked, humbled and compelled to have recourse to the generosity of his mother. On one occasion, harassed over a crying debt, he misappropriated a sum of money entrusted to him by a friend, and he nearly went mad at the tergiversations of Ancelle and the hesitations of his mother. Baudelaire knew that, at that moment, he was facing prison. The friend, to whom Baudelaire made a full confession, gave him time until his mother, at last grasping the situation, rushed him the necessary amount. Baudelaire, however, assured her that these incidents and these demands would not continue, and that he would, somehow, positively straighten out his affairs And with the real suffering, even illness, that "the lack of luxuries" and necessities was now bringing upon him, he nevertheless felt that he was enjoying something like happiness in the somewhat brilliant presence of Madame Sabatier and in the nearness of his mother.

Furthermore, his confidence in his future was receiving renewed stimulus in the further progress he was making with his work. First of all, with Monselet and Champfleury, he had brought out a magazine called *La Semaine théâtrale,* which, although it lasted only nine weeks, kept his name before the public. Then he had been asked to do an article on the pictures at the Exposition Universelle in 1855.

He attacked this assignment with appetite, for, next to writing poetry, he preferred art criticism. In this article, he avoided the flashing wit, the cogent thrusts of his "Salons"

of 1845 and 1846. He took the more serene tone of the arrived critic, set out brilliantly his attitude toward art, and went in for a more extended analysis of the artists who were exhibiting. He at once abjured all connection with any "system" or school of criticism. A system excludes too much; for, in the beautiful, there is always decidedly more than can be accounted for in the rule. Moreover, temperamentally, he could not "close himself up" in a system. He was not going to look simply for technique but for "feeling, morality and pleasure." Art was not for him a dexterous manipulation but a magical operation; and he felt that no one had the right to determine the methods by which the magician had been successful.

He dedicated, by preference, the bulk of his discussion to the works of Delacroix and Ingres. He found Delacroix as superior as ever in his power to achieve, without the technical meretriciousness of the times, sublime effects "through a profound and entire harmony of subject, design and color," mingling drama and revery, for example, so well in his portrait of the *Doge Marino Faliero,* and achieving in *La Justice de Trajan* such an effect of pomp and tumult, that, even after he left them, the pictures "haunted, followed and tormented" him.

But, with Ingres, Baudelaire found it necessary to make a revaluation. Previously, it was true, he had considered Ingres superior for his handling of color and for his superb line. But now he found him singularly shallow as compared with Girodet, and pointedly lacking in movement, as compared with his master, David. Baudelaire began to feel that Ingres had suppressed his models too much. He sensed, for example, in the two *Odalisques,* for all their little touches of Chinese and Persian effect and color, a coldness, a resignation, an ideal composed part of lovely flesh and part of death-like quiet which filled him with uneasiness.

XV

WHILE THIS ARTICLE was not received with the enthusiasm which followed the "Salons," it served to draw public attention to him as a critic of fresh and mature powers. He was encouraged to renewed effort in his writing; and, even if the intensity with which he worked further affected his health and upset his nerves, he was satisfied that he was ultimately achieving what he wished.

He worked, however, with increasing difficulty. He found that, in spite of intense application, there were long blank periods in which, with the best of intentions, he could not make himself say the things he wished. This "deterioration of his will," as he called it, this inability to bring together quickly thought and articulation, upset him. It terrified him all the more because it was, in part, this sort of doubt of his powers which had just impelled Gérard de Nerval to commit suicide. He was further hindered in his tremendous effort at this time not only to complete projected plays and stories of his own but to turn out daily for *Le Pays* a translation of a story by Poe, by the necessity of moving from hotel to hotel to avoid the importunities of his creditors and the nagging of landlords. At one time, he had six addresses in six months.

His nerves suffered, too, from these frequent irritations and from the enormous sense of loneliness which now more and more took hold of him. Except for his infrequent attendance at Mürger's Mondays, rare visits to Madame Sabatier's salon, and at this time only occasional visits to his mother, he scarcely went anywhere. This extreme feeling of loneliness had seemed always to follow him. He had felt it first profoundly on the marriage of the Aupicks. At Le Collège Royal at Lyon, where, upon the transfer of General Aupick to Lyon in 1831, Baudelaire had been sent as a boarding student "for his own good," he complained in a letter to his mother that, while there was any amount of "common sense" at the school, there was an enormous "absence of love." He added in the letter that he must try to be content because "this is what you wished." At Le Collège Royal, he took a kind of sombre refuge in solitariness; and he felt even more profoundly lonely at Le Lycée Louis-le-Grand in Paris, where he was under the influence of the "grand, melodious and unassuageable melancholy," of Alfred de Vigny and Lamartine. Upon his trip to the Pyrenees with his step-father in 1839, which had been arranged by General Aupick in an effort "to bring him to his senses," Baudelaire experienced, by way of the majestic aloofness of the clouds, mountains and valleys, an immense loneliness and silence that made him wish, as he expressed it in a poem written then, "to run away." In the midst of his tremendous effort in 1855, he would feel suddenly and entirely cut off from all love and peace and with no one to turn to anywhere. He was hungry for the God he was otherwise so aware of and was now expressing so clearly in his poems; but it did not yet occur to him to receive Him fully. Instead, on these occasions, he would berate his mother for her "abandonment" of him, plunge into some casual debauch, or shut himself up for days to rewrite and polish his work with patient intensity.

xvi

HE NOW THOUGHT that he was ready to launch his book of poetry. It was the publication of this, he felt, which would give him the greatest satisfaction. He had worked these poems over and over for more than ten years, adding only a few new ones. He was sure of their perfection, sure that their mordant substance and their unusual treatment would give him a large public and a high place in French literature. Heretofore he had sent only a few of them to the reviews. He began to send them out now.

Le Messager de l'assemblée had accepted nine immediately. Among these were "La Mort des amants" with its exquisite music:

> Nous aurons des lits pleins d'odeurs légères
> Des divans profonds comme des tombeaux; [1]

and "La Mort des artistes" with its description of the hellish struggle to achieve beauty and its statement of the hope of the defeated artist to reach it after death. *L'Anthologie des poètes de l'amour* had included in its collection his rather long poem, "Lesbos," which, in its bold celebration of Sappho, of the hollow eyes and lovely pallor, who was plunged "in the black mystery"

> Des rires effrénés mêlés aux sombres pleurs [2]

gave the public a taste of his startling originality.

---

[1] We shall have beds full of light scents
Divans as deep as tombs.
    "La Mort des amants."
[2] Of wild laughter mingled with sombre tears.
    "Lesbos."

"Le Reniement de Saint Pierre," had appeared in *La Revue de Paris*. In this ironic poem of "revolt," in which he asked, speaking of Jesus,

> Lorsque tu vis cracher sur ta divinité
> La crapule du corps de garde et des cuisines,
> Et lorsque tu sentis s'enfoncer les épines
> Dans ton crâne où vivait l'immense Humanité,
>
> .   .   .   .
>
> Rêvais-tu de ces jours si brillants et si beaux
> Où tu vins pour remplir l'éternelle promesse,
> Où tu foulais, monté sur ta douce ânesse
> Des chemins tout jonchés de fleurs et de rameaux? [1]

and in which he permitted Peter, "full of anger and ignorance" to explain his denial of Christ.

Le Magasin des familles had taken two poems, "L'Ame du vin" and "Châtiment de l'orgueuil." "L'Ame du vin" simply celebrates wine for its renewal of the weary. "Châtiment de l'orgueuil" relates how,

> En ces temps merveilleux où la Théologie
> Fleurit avec le plus de sève et d'énergie, [2]

[1] When Thou didst see them spew on Thy divinity,
The swine of the guard-room and the kitchens,
When Thou didst feel the thorns thrust
In Thy skull where lived immense Humanity,

.   .   .   .

Didst Thou dream then of lovely, shining days
When Thou didst come to bring eternal promise,
When Thou didst ride upon Thy gentle donkey,
The roads scattered with blossoms and with palms?
"Le Reniement de Saint Pierre."

[2] In those wondrous times when Theology
Flourished with more verve and energy,
"Châtiment de l'orgueuil."

a doctor of theology, proud of the logic by which he demonstrated the glory of Christ, boasts that, with the same powers, he could just as well have demolished Him. Immediately upon this show of bravado, the doctor's reason left him. Chaos took the place of his logic, and "silence and night installed themselves in him." For some reason, the editor, Léo Lespès, found it necessary to attach a note to the poems, saying, "These two unpublished pieces are taken from a book entitled Les Limbes, which will appear soon and which is destined to represent the agitations and melancholies of modern youth."

Buloz, who had accepted eighteen poems for *La Revue des Deux-Mondes,* had also found it necessary to add a note which puzzled and considerably angered Baudelaire. The group of poems bearing the title of *Les Fleurs du mal,* which Hippolyte Babou had suggested, contained some of the most beautifully done and most striking of his work. It began with the celebrated "Au Lecteur" in which Baudelaire states his view of the world. In this poem the religious theme continues, as it is to shine by implication or by clear statement in nearly all the poems. The Satanism, the evil, the celebration of the senses, are magnificently and powerfully expressed; but they are there only as foils: one cannot but feel their inadequacy and their failure in his life. In this particular poem, in which he keeps insisting that

Nos péchés sont têtus, nos repentirs sont lâches [1]

he sees error, stupidity, sin occupying the mind and wearing out the body. The Devil rules the world. Daily, without horror, we take another step toward hell, clinging to sin like "a debauchee to the worn breast of an aged whore." Our banal and pitiful destiny is peopled with demons, among

[1] Our sins are stubborn, our repentance cowardly
"Au Lecteur."

which is one that "would swallow the world in a yawn"—
Boredom, that "delicate monster" whom you knew well,
"Hypocritical Reader, My Brother." In "La Cloche fêlée," he
describes how, upon hearing deep in the night the beautiful
and "religious cry" of the carillons,

> . . . qui chantent dans la brume,[1]

he tries to make his own song reach their profundity and
perfection; but his voice is like the feeble call of a wounded
soldier, who, from under the pile of dead, is trying to extricate himself "with immense effort." The will to God is
clearly expressed, and the weakness of his flesh. "Un Voyage
à Cythère" removes the illusions from love. He looks coldly
at Cythera. It is indeed, "a poor land,"

> Un désert rocailleux troublé par des cris aigres,[2]

where, symbolically, in the figure of a decaying body on a
gibbet, he sees himself, in "expiation of sins" which have
even forbidden him the tomb; and he prays, "O Lord, give
me the strength and the courage to contemplate my heart
and my body without disgust." There is scarcely a better
expression of feeble humanity and Christian effort.

The note which Buloz appended explained that the magazine was printing these poems because it was "favorable to
the spirit of experiment in the most diverse directions." The
editor insisted that the magazine did not share "certain violences and weaknesses"; but that these were "one of the
signs of the times." Further, he felt that by giving these
poems this publicity, the magazine "was not only encourag-
ing, but, inspiring, true talent to free itself, to strengthen
itself, by extending its paths and expanding its horizons."

---

[1] . . . which sing in the fog
"La Cloche fêlée."
[2] A rocky desert troubled by piercing cries
"Un Voyage à Cythère."

Baudelaire simply could not understand what Buloz was talking about; but the attack written by Louis Goudall which appeared later in *Le Figaro* could not be misunderstood. "Baudelaire is detestable," it said. "He has mystified Paris for ten years. Paris is extremely stupid. Baudelaire has a heart-breaking poverty of ideas; a language, ignorant and colorless. All he can talk about is worms, dead bodies, monsters, murderers and tombs. Expression of our time, indeed!"

On the other hand, he had been encouraged, in spite of Buloz's remarks in *La Revue des Deux-Mondes*; for it was the known policy of that magazine to print no one but "arrived" poets. Furthermore, he was delighted with Flaubert's judgment of his poems. Upon receiving from Baudelaire a copy of *La Revue des Deux-Mondes* containing the group, Flaubert wrote immediately that he admired the poems profoundly, particularly "Tristesses de la lune," and "Un Voyage à Cythère," adding, "You sing of the flesh so well, without loving it."

In addition, his translation of a group of Poe's stories to which he gave the title of *Histoires extraordinaires,* published by Michel Lévy, was receiving, on the whole, excellent notices. It is true that he was disappointed that Sainte-Beuve, to whom he had sent a copy at *Le Constitutionnel,* hoping he might find time to say a few words about it, had thanked him for the book, said he was very busy, and had never reviewed it. It is true also that Edouard Duranty of *Le Figaro* had written: "Baudelaire clings to Poe in order to enjoy a part of his glory"; but the general critical tone was of high approval. In the same *Figaro,* Legendre had written that Baudelaire was "a clear intelligence, brilliant, sharp as a sword and philosophical." In *Le Moniteur,* Edouard Thierry had praised him highly. This was followed by apparently sincere applause from current popular critics like Charles Philarète and Victor Fournel. Even Armand de Pontmartin, that excessive "moralist of the drawing-rooms" had had nothing but good to say of his translation of Poe. He was, therefore, on the whole, encouraged to go on with the completion of *Les Fleurs du mal,* the title which he decided to use for his book, because it described eminently both the substance and the purpose of the poems; and he set out to find a publisher.

xvii

AT THIS TIME, General Aupick died. Baudelaire was shocked, not so much by the fact of his death, but because he felt somehow defrauded by it; for he could no longer prove to the General the worth of his talent. In 1851, Maxime du Camp, whose opinions on literature and public affairs the General respected, was passing through Constantinople and visited the Aupicks. To Madame Aupick's timid inquiry whether he thought Baudelaire had talent, his half answer had assured the General to the contrary. On all the copies of his articles, poems and stories which Baudelaire consistently sent his mother with the warning to take good care of them "because they would be valuable," General Aupick had made no comment whatever that reached Baudelaire. It is assumed that he never even read them; but it is supposed that the somewhat scandalous reaction that followed Goudall's remarks in so widely a circulated paper as *Le Figaro,* had been a blow which had seriously affected the General's health. Indeed, it is presumed by some to have been one of the causes of his death.

In any case, Baudelaire hastened to do what he considered the suitable thing. He suddenly felt that the General's death was "a call to order"; that it was time for him to take command of his life, of his tangled affairs, bring order to them and, above all, to look out for his mother for whom he now felt entirely responsible. He went to the funeral for the major purpose of consoling his mother; but he could not get near her for the horde of the General's friends and admirers

who constantly surrounded her. Most of these scarcely spoke
to him. The only person who spoke to him with any degree
of friendliness was the courtly Monsieur Jacquotot, who had
said to him gently, "I suppose you will now come to live
with your mother." Later, touched by this, Baudelaire tried
to have his mother agree to take the management of the
small fortune that remained to him out of the hands of
Ancelle and to give it to Monsieur Jacquotot. Monsieur
Emon, a captain of artillery, former aide-de-camp of General
Aupick, and now executor of the General's estate, turned his
back on him. For the next few weeks, Baudelaire, anxious
to be of service to his mother in the thousand little matters
which must have required her attention on this occasion,
could scarcely get to her for Monsieur Emon. Monsieur
Emon seemed to wish to protect her from him.

xviii

MEANTIME, HE CONTINUED his search for a publisher. Michel Lévy declined at once to take a chance with the book. Sainte-Beuve, from whom Baudelaire, with humble indirection, requested an introduction to his publisher, responded that, in these matters, he must be excused; because he had made it a point never to make recommendations of this sort. It was then that the father of his friend, Auguste Poulet-Malassis, had died, leaving to his son a newspaper and publishing house in Alençon.

Poulet-Malassis had taste and culture. When his father died, he felt that he could expand the business. With the financial collaboration of his brother-in-law, Debroise, he decided not only to bring out *Le Journal d'Alençon* and to do some modest provincial publishing, but to publish in Paris where he opened, in the Rue de Richelieu, an exquisite office and book shop decorated on the panels with the portraits of the most important people he was presenting. He had decided that a renaissance in good typography was due. Good typography had been somewhat in abeyance since 1848; and he felt that for the modest sum of four or five francs, he could bring out a volume on good paper, well bound, with titles and initial letters in red, with decorative tail-pieces and with a clear type which could well compare with the work of Perrin in Lyon or of Hérissey at Evreux. His was an ancient family of printers whose long established house held a license from Marguérite de Valois. Poulet-Malassis, furthermore, knew and loved the trade profoundly.

It was, therefore, with confidence and hope that he began business in Paris.

When Baudelaire heard that Poulet-Malassis, or "Coco Malperché," as he called him, had inherited the business, he presented to him the proposition of publishing *Les Fleurs du mal*. Their association at L'École des Chartes had begun a lasting intimacy between them. Poulet-Malassis had a turn for eighteenth century philosophy, was a professed atheist, and liked to torment Baudelaire with his anti-clerical wit and flashing Voltaireisms. Baudelaire would either retort in a fury of profanity, cursing "that damned wretch, Voltaire," or would reply with such a profound knowledge of Catholic theology and with such patient and learned argument that, as Asselineau observed, if one had heard and had not seen Baudelaire on these occasions, one would have taken him for a doctor of the Church.

In any case, their intimacy inclined Poulet-Malassis to accept Baudelaire's proposition. Furthermore, Poulet-Malassis had long admired what he had seen privately of Baudelaire's work, indeed, had already done something to spread Baudelaire's reputation. His brother-in-law, Debroise, had hedged a little. He preferred, in the first place, to stay out of the Paris field. If Paris was inevitable, then he preferred to republish fine editions of well-known writers. Under his influence, the firm republished the poetry of Sainte-Beuve, the *Émaux et Camées* of Théophile Gautier, and some minor prose of Balzac. Under the more modern influence of Poulet-Malassis, it brought out *Les Poèmes Barbares* of Leconte de Lisle, *Les Poèmes Funambulesques* of Théodore de Banville and some prose of Champfleury. The decision of Poulet-Malassis to publish Baudelaire met further resistance from Debroise because Debroise did not care personally very much for Baudelaire and was not, on the whole, particularly won over by his poetry. But the decision of Poulet-Malassis prevailed. He announced in *Le Journal de la librairie* that he was bringing out shortly a first edition of 1300 copies of *Les Fleurs du mal* on vellum. He made a contract with Baudelaire, promising him twenty-five centimes for every copy sold; and in the early months of 1857, the printery at Alençon, under the direction of Debroise, went to work on the proofs.

xix

WITH ENTHUSIASM, Baudelaire pushed aside everything he was doing, except work for *Le Pays* and work on *Les Nouvelles Histoires extraordinaires,* another volume of Poe's stories which Michel Lévy was to publish shortly, and set about putting his poems in their final form.

The manuscript was in the hands of Poulet-Malassis by February 10, 1857. Baudelaire's anxieties began at once. He began worrying about the form which his dedication of the book to Théophile Gautier should take. He could not conceive the full value of his poems or entirely detect their weaknesses until he saw them in print. With his customary fastidiousness, he attacked the proofs which began slowly coming to him from Alençon. The task was all the more difficult because he still had to get in at *Le Pays* his daily translation of a story by Poe. He agonized over the dedication. He decided he would consult Gautier himself about it. So involved did he become with his dedication and his proofs, that he missed for the first time getting his daily translation to *Le Pays.* Friction with Debroise began almost immediately. Baudelaire wrote him a terrified letter. "What has happened to the package of proofs which you claim you sent me? I am sure they must be lost in the mail." But no, they arrive safely. Now, "everything will go smoothly." But he writes back to Debroise almost at once, "Do you have to use such long queer-looking quotes? For heaven's sake, put some space between title and poem. Don't be stingy with your paper. I am sure you must be angry with me for my delay in sending back the first package of proofs; but you will see that I am right with my carefulness."

Then he began complaining about the size of the type. He insisted upon a larger size in the dedication, which he had finally decided upon. Baudelaire had at first thought that, in addition to the dedication, some prefatory remarks might be necessary. He had written in his first dedication that though he was asking Gautier to be god-parent of *Les Fleurs du mal,* he must not be thought "so unworthy of the name of poet as to believe that these sickly flowers deserved Gautier's noble patronage." "I know," he had begun, "that in the etherial realm of true poetry, Evil does not exist any more than Good." But Gautier had advised him that this dedication was "too much of a programme," and Baudelaire had decided not to use it.

Baudelaire insisted to Poulet-Malassis that everything he had changed in the proofs must be changed in the final printing; that he would pay personally for new forms. Then he did not sleep for several nights because the mails were slow in getting back a package of proofs to Debroise. The delays of Baudelaire began to annoy Poulet-Malassis. He wants the whole business of the proofs finished in two more weeks. Baudelaire exclaims, "Can I help it, if my eye is good and your compositors are imbeciles?" He insists that his care is a good guarantee. He wants a word changed that will upset a whole line of type. He wants to change, in the poem, "Spleen," "l'ennui fils de la morne incuriosité" to "l'ennui, fruit de la morne incuriosité." Debroise rages. Baudelaire declares that the change adds immense value to the line. Furthermore, he can no longer bear the mistakes the compositors are making. He will come to Alençon himself.

If it had not been for the placating and softening influence of Poulet-Malassis' mother, it is probable that the whole affair would have been given up. As it was, relations were considerably strained because Baudelaire all during his stay kept insisting on more changes and revision of changes, regardless of time and expense. He wanted his book to be perfect.

The book was now taking its final form. There were frequent changes and counter-changes in the order of the poems and considerable bickering about the typography of the table of contents, the material and color of the cover. But by the end of April he had sent in all the proofs; and, in a sort of celebration he ate and drank up "in five days" all the money he had made out of his translations for *Le Pays*.

He then set about choosing his critics. He sent, first of all, an especially bound volume to Sainte-Beuve, who accepted it with thanks, explained that, as usual, he was tremendously occupied, and never made any effort to review it in *Le Constitutionnel*. Baudelaire counted on an appreciative article by Edouard Thierry at *Le Moniteur*. He felt, further, that after his friendly difference with Barbey d'Aurevilly in the matter of Poe, he would be able to depend on a somewhat more responsible attitude this time in *Le Pays*. Asselineau, who was on the editorial staff of *La Revue française,* would surely do a review for him in that periodical. As for the rest of the press and important literary magazines, he was certain that, while he did not have everywhere a direct influence, Asselineau and other friends would make efforts for him, and the book would speak for itself.

Toward the end of June, the printing and binding were finally done. While it was an excellent job of the printer's art, from its somewhat vibrantly humble dedication to that "impeccable poet," "that dear friend and master, Théophile Gautier," of "these sick flowers," to the last ironically hopeful lines of "La Mort des artistes," Baudelaire was still nervous.

The feel of the book excited him. Everything was in it

that he wished and it was all himself. It contained the fruit of his fastidiousness: the exact word charged with the right tone, with its special contribution to the music of the line, to the harmony of the whole. The lines and poems were muscular and clean-cut. There was no flabbiness, none of the "vegetable meandering" that he so much detested in Alfred de Musset. Every poem moved inevitably to its clear conclusion, its music, even with sudden changes in timbre and tempo, always in control; its emotion, even with frequent bursts of lyric despair or hope, never out of guidance of a cold intelligence. He had chosen titles, as he had told Poulet-Malassis, which would catch attention "like firecrackers." And then, in these poems, he had spoken of himself with perfect frankness. The book would succeed, he felt, because it was classic in form yet rich and sparkling with an originality and a personalism unknown to French letters.

Against a background of that "great whore," Paris, where at the hour of dawn

> . . . l'essaim des rêves malfaisants
> Tord sur leurs oreillers les bruns adolescents;
> Où, comme un oeil sanglant qui palpite et qui bouge,
> La lampe sur le jour fait une tache rouge;
> Où l'âme, sous le poids du corps revêche et lourd,
> Imite les combats de la lampe et du jour.[1]

against a background of nature, which was so beautiful in its "Swedenborgian correspondences"; which,

---

[1] . . . the swarm of wicked dreams
Twist brown adolescents on their pillows;
Where like a bloody eye that flutters and moves,
The lamp upon the daylight makes a red stain,
Where the soul, under the weight of stubborn, heavy flesh
Reflects the combat of the lamp against the day.
"Crépuscule du matin."

Comme de longs echos qui de loin se confondent
Dans une ténébreuse et profonde unité,
Vaste comme la nuit et comme la clarté,[1]

was so eloquent in its forms and yet so reticent, so formidable and terrifying in its destructiveness, he had, in these
poems, moved between the extreme of reality and the extreme of the ideal, seeking "the light and the key" and some
ultimate repose for the confused and restless spirit. He begins with his "shadowy youth lit here and there by flashes";
rebukes, as in "Bénédiction," his mother for her denial of
him as a poet; and feels that from his youngest days the
world—except for the consolations of Mariette, to whom
"this October we must take some flowers, for the dead still
suffer pain"—has been a place of reptiles, peopled with
demons and motivated by the Devil.

C'est un univers morne à l'horizon plombé,
Où nagent dans la nuit l'horreur et le blasphème.[2]

It had appeared to him a place of boredom, enigma, ugliness
and decay, made the more terrifying by the passage of time
"with its insect voice," telling off the minutes to his own
death. He had recorded that, although beauty had given him
glimpses of the infinite,

Par delà le soleil, par delà les éthèrs
Par delà les confins des sphères étoilées,[3]

[1] Like long echoes which are confused afar
In a shadowy and profound unity,
Vast as the dark and as the light.
   "Correspondances."
[2] It is a mournful universe with leaden sky
Where move in night, horror and blasphemy.
   "De Profundis Clamavi."
[3] Beyond the sun, beyond the ether,
Beyond the confines of the starry spheres.
   "Élévation."

and had made the "universe less hideous and the moments
less heavy," it was, after all, "a dream of stone" against
which the artist could destroy himself. He had revealed how,
with Jeanne,

> Toi qui, forte comme un troupeau
> De démons, vins, folle et parée,
> De mon esprit humilié
> Faire ton lit et ton domaine; [1]

he had sought in evil a solution which had brought him only
remorse and disgust; how, with Madame Sabatier,

> . . . un vent frais dans un ciel clair,[2]

he was seeking a kind of liberation from the body. And yet
"the gulf that swallowed all the dead" still remained,

> . . . cette immense nuit semblable au vieux Chaos.[3]

And, in his confusion of soul, he had recorded how he had
preferred Satan to God, preferred "the certainty of hell to
the certainty of annihilation"; preferred, on that day when
Satan's "forehead would break out in leaves" to repose with
him under the Tree of Knowledge, rather than suffer, waiting the judgment of an inscrutable God. In a Byronic moment of revolt he had cried out at the "complacence of God"
before the suffering of humanity, had written:

[1] You who, strong as a flock
  Of demons, came, wild and jewelled
  To make of my humiliated spirit
  Your bed and your domain.
            "Le Vampire."
[2] A cool wind in a clear sky
            "A celle qui est trop gaie."
[3] . . . that immense night like old Chaos.
            "De Profundis Clamavi."

> Race de Caïn, au ciel monte
> Et sur la terre jette Dieu! [1]

Yet, it occurred to him that if God had compelled his spirit to suffer so much, it must have been to wash him clean of his impurity and he exclaims:

> Soyez béni, mon Dieu, qui donnez la souffrance
> Comme un divin remède à nos impuretés [2]

And, seeing the blind pass by with their eyes turned to the sky,

> Au ciel; on ne les voit jamais vers les pavés,[3]

"as if they looked far off," he, wondered whether, perhaps, he "had not been more confused than they," when he had asked, "Why do they look into the sky?"

He had worked so hard and long at the book, and it was so much a part of him, that to let it go ultimately was like tearing away a part of himself. About the last week in June, however, review copies had been circulated and the book was put on sale first in the book-shop of Poulet-Malassis in the Rue de Richelieu.

---

[1] Race of Cain, to heaven rise
  And cast down God upon the earth!
        "Abel et Caïn."
[2] Blessed be God who giveth pain
  As a divine remedy to our impurity
        "Bénédiction."
[3] To heaven; one never sees them turn toward earth.
        "Les Aveugles."

XX

THE FIRST DISQUIETING news to Baudelaire came from Barbey d'Aurevilly at *Le Pays*. According to a note written in haste by him, word had been sent to him from the inner offices of his paper that the book was not to be reviewed. Closely following this note came another from Asselineau at *La Revnue française,* telling him that his review was stopped after it had already been set in type. On the fifth of July, an article appeared in *Le Figaro* presumably inspired by Bilhault, Minister of the Interior, and written by Gustave Bourdin, son-in-law of the owner, Villemessant. It said in part that, in this book, "the odious rubs shoulders with the ignoble and repulsiveness is side by side with impurity. Never has one seen so many breasts bitten in so few pages; never has there been such a parade of demons, devils, foetuses, cats and vermin. The book is a hospital full of all the madnesses of the spirit, all the rottenness of the heart. Nothing can justify anyone for publishing a book of so many monstrosities." The article had introduced Baudelaire as "the Messiah of a cénacle which calls Hugo a chancre, Christ a tramp, and Louis Napoleon an idiot." The next day Baudelaire received from Brussels a copy of *Le Journal de Bruxelles* which called *Les Fleurs du mal* "a dirty book from which quotation is impossible." Habans, the same day, wrote in *Le Figaro* that "the eagle is nothing but a fly from whom all his friends are fleeing, holding their noses."

Asselineau warned Baudelaire that he had heard that the government intended seizing the entire edition. In a frenzy,

Baudelaire wrote on July 11 to Poulet-Malassis to hide all the copies. The seizure had not yet been attempted; but within a day the government summoned Debroise, Poulet-Malassis and Baudelaire before Charles Camusat Busseroles, le juge d'instruction, for a hearing at which it was formally decided to put them on trial for an attack upon religion and public morals.

Baudelaire was stunned. His mother, who had been terrified by many of the poems, particularly by "Le Reniement de Saint Pierre," feared the worst. It seemed incredible not only that he had been misunderstood but that on the basis of that misunderstanding he was to be put on public trial. He was told that the government which had gagged the political press had to show impartiality by putting pressure on book publishers and literary men who had been enjoying, almost unmolested, freedom of expression. He was told further, that the government was angry that in its first serious efforts to suppress a literary man, Flaubert, it had failed; and that now it must do something to satisfy the grumblings of suppressed newspaper editors. This explanation did not satisfy Baudelaire, who was resentful, angry and desperately chagrined that this had happened to the book on which he had counted to establish definitely his literary reputation.

He slept now even less than before, sometimes falling across the bed at noon into a sort of stupor after being awake all night. He scarcely ate. He turned helplessly in all directions, not certain how to grapple with this ghastly situation. He was certain that something had to be done and that he had to do it because Poulet-Malassis and Debroise had lost their heads altogether.

Meantime, Edouard Thierry's article appeared on July 14 in *Le Moniteur*. It emphasized Baudelaire's qualities and his hatred of evil. It was astonishing that this article in favor of Baudelaire should appear in a government-controlled paper. Bilhault, Minister of the Interior, was enraged. In *Le Présent,* Frédéric Dulamon also defended Baudelaire, saying "his description of evil was made to inspire us with a desire to return to good."

Baudelaire hastily wrote to Fould, Minister of State, quoting the sentiments of Thierry, emphasizing particularly the statement that "Baudelaire's unhappiness and despair" were "sufficient morality." Baudelaire added that since Monsieur Fould had interceded so successfully before the Council of State in the matter of a pension for his mother upon the death of General Aupick; and since, furthermore, in his position, he was "the natural protector of artists"; he hoped that Monsieur Fould would come to his assistance in this matter.

Before Baudelaire could receive a reply to this letter, he was informed that the government was going to try him particularly for these poems: the two "Femmes damnées," "Lesbos," "Les métamorphoses du Vampire," "A Celle qui est trop gaie," "Tout entière," "Les Bijoux" and "Le Reniement de Saint Pierre." Baudelaire feverishly took command of the defense. He forbade Poulet-Malassis to interfere or "to gossip" or to do anything without his advice. For some reason, possibly on the reputation of his father or for some supposed influence with the Emperor, Baudelaire selected Chaix d'Est-Ange, the younger, to defend him. Then tensely, he set about what he thought would be some effective string-pulling, solicitations of influence, for the trial which was to take place on the twentieth of August in the Criminal Court.

The whole affair was so unreal, so much a reversal of the situation which he had expected, that he really did not know what he was doing. He first appealed to his mother, asking her if she could get a word for him to Mérimée or the Princess Mathilde. Then he ran about asking literary friends what to do. Gautier could only give him some vague counsel to the effect that he should say that his purpose had been "to listen, to translate subtle confidences of depraved passions and odd hallucinations of a fixed idea turning to madness." After laying frantic siege to Sainte-Beuve's offices, begging for "only three minutes" of the great man's time, he was unable to see him at this critical moment. He ultimately received a letter which advised him to urge his lawyer to plead before the court that "everything in the realm of poetry had been taken. Lamartine had taken the heavens; Victor Hugo, the earth; Laprade, the forests, and Alfred de Musset, passion. Others had taken the home, rural life. Théophile Gautier had taken Spain. What remained? What Baudelaire took. He was forced to it." Even though it was from Sainte-Beuve, this system of reasoning was so obscure and so questionable that Baudelaire did not dare use it.

He set out first of all to discover who his judges were to be. He found that Dupaty was to be President of the Court; Pinard, the Imperial Prosecutor, and Delesvaux, Ponton d'Amécourt and Nacquart were to be the judges. He somehow got hold of the novelist, Brücker, and urged him to see if he could reach Dupaty. He had decided that one must defeat the world by the world's own methods. He urged Chaix d'Est-Ange to cite "with disgust and horror," the "filth"—"les bonnes vieilles saletés," particularly "Le Bon Dieu," "Margot," and "Jeanneton"—of Béranger, to whom the Empire had just given a public funeral of honor. He urged him not to overlook "La Chute des Anges." Then he solicited the assistance of Madame Sabatier. He wrote to her, "Flaubert had for him the Empress. I need you. See if you can get a sensible word to these big-wigs."

Madame Sabatier, who, in spite of the various associations which she enjoyed in her salon, was unable to reach Baudelaire's judges in any way, had by this time discovered that it was Baudelaire who had been sending her those subtle and stimulating poems. She was, above all, somehow thrilled that two of them, "A Celle qui est trop gaie" and "Tout entière," had been condemned by the government. The notoriety which this action gave the poems and the very special kind of adoration expressed in them, made her feel more now than just a comrade at the dinner table. And, while she could not reach the judges, she put herself out in many ways to attempt to encourage Baudelaire.

xxi

BAUDELAIRE WAS IN A FEVER on the day of the trial. Impeccably, but as usual somewhat oddly, dressed, he sat outwardly calm and impassive, his emotion shown only by his excessive pallor and his tenseness. The court-room was a drawing by Daumier. The faces of the judges seemed to him "as ugly as their souls." Nacquart, Delesvaux and Ponton d'Amécourt chatted aimiably together, "almost giggled." Dupaty, the President, kept looking at his watch, and, distractedly, at the door, as if he had some more pressing matter than this to attend to. And, to Baudelaire's greater irritation, through the court-room, with an air at once of familiarity and importance, moved the florid Ancelle in the frock-coat and wing collar which he wore as Mayor of Neuilly. Baudelaire could have strangled him. Ancelle went from person to person in the court-room, bowing and talking with the greatest familiarity, although this was the first time he had met any of them. On the news of Baudelaire's trial, Ancelle had rushed to Paris to be of assistance. Baudelaire agonized over what he might be saying, and prayed that the session might begin and silence him.

To Baudelaire's surprise, Pinard, the Imperial Prosecutor, appeared ill-at-ease, apologetic. Baudelaire was convinced at first that he must somehow have been reached, if not by Madame Sabatier, perhaps by Barbey d'Aurevilly or by Brücker. Pinard began by assuring the court that he did not wish "Monsieur Baudelaire's head." He observed in the most conciliatory manner that, while there were expressions like,

Tu me rapporteras tes seins stigmatisés;[1]

and

. . . Saint Antoine a vu. . . .
Les seins nus et pourprés de ses tentations,[2]

in "Les Femmes damnées," these two poems of the same
name were not sufficiently obscene for the correction of the
court. He lingered somewhat unhappily over "Le Reniement
de Saint-Pierre," declaring, with the same lack of personal
conviction, that there might be in this poem sufficient violence against God to consider it blasphemous, particularly
in the conclusion, where Baudelaire has Peter, revolted by
the treatment of Jesus, say:

—Certes, je sortirai, quant à moi, satisfait,
D'un monde où l'action n'est pas la soeur du rêve;
Puissé-je user du glaive et périr par le glaive! [3]

He then turned to the other poems. He felt that in "Les
Bijoux" expressions like:

La très chère . . .
. . . n'avait gardé que ses bijoux sonores.
. . . et se laissait aimer,
. . . et la candeur unie à la lubricité
Donnait un charme neuf.

* * * *

[1] You will bring back to me your tormented breasts
"Femmes damnées."
[2] Saint Anthony saw . . .
The naked and purple breasts of his temptation
"Femmes damnées."
[3] Certainly, I shall leave, content,
A world where action is not sister to the dream;
Let me use the sword and perish by it.
"Le Reniement de Saint Pierre."

and all her charms,

> Ces grappes de ma vigne,
> S'avançaient plus câlins que les anges du mal,
> Pour troubler le repos où mon âme était mise,[1]

were certainly more than suggestive; that in "Le Léthé," and "Lesbos," sentiments like:

> J'étalerai mes baisers sans remord
> Sur ton beau corps; [2]

and

> Les filles aux yeux creux, de leurs corps amoureuses,
> Caressent les fruits mûrs de leur nubilité . . . ; [3]

and the speech of the woman in "Les métamorphoses du Vampire," in which she boasts that when she abandons herself to sin,

> Les anges impuissants se damneraient pour moi! [4]

might certainly not be considered clean literature. As for "Tout entière" and "A celle qui est trop gaie," the idea of

---

[1] My beloved,
Kept only her sonorous jewels.
. . . She let herself be loved,
And candor, united to lubricity, gave a new charm.

. . . . .

Those grapes of my vine,
Advanced more sly than the angels of evil
To trouble my soul. . . .
    "Les Bijoux."

[2] I shall scatter my kisses without remorse
Over your lovely flesh. . . .
    "Le Léthé."

[3] Girls with hollow eyes,
Caress the ripe fruit of their nubility.
    "Lesbos."

[4] Impotent angels would damn themselves for me!
    "Métamorphoses du Vampire."

hovering over "the pink and black" beauty of a woman, hesitating to select

> Parmi toutes les belles choses
> Dont est fait son enchantement. . . .[1]

her most seductive charm; and the philosophy of wishing to degrade that beauty by the wish

> . . . infuser mon poison,[2]

exhibited perhaps a kind of perversity which possibly should not be made public. With that, Pinard, scarcely lifting his eyes and with a depreciating smile to the court, rested his case.

Baudelaire raged silently, not only because Pinard had not troubled to go beyond words, phrases, isolated images and sentiments to the full meaning of the poem, but also because, in a Paris teeming with a literature, far from surreptitious, of admitted obscenity, the government had decided that the poems over which he had labored to no such purpose should publicly be pawed over and examined minutely for lubricity. Furthermore, upon the publication in magazines of "Lesbos" in 1850 and of "Le Reniement de Saint Pierre" in 1852, not a word had been uttered against them by the authorities.

Chaix d'Est-Ange, without any effort to follow Baudelaire's advice to quote "the dirtiness of his contemporaries" or to plead that each poem should be considered in its whole effect and the book "in its ensemble," began taking up, one by one, the words and phrases which Pinard had so apologetically challenged, defending them, going into dictionary meanings and into the possible salacious effectiveness of the

---

[1] Among all the lovely things
Which make her charm. . . .
"A celle qui est trop gaie."
[2] To infuse my poison.
"A celle qui est trop gaie."

sentiments in question. He argued, furthermore, without apparent interest and practically inaudibly. Lançon, the attorney for Poulet-Malassis and Debroise, was just as negative.

The judges decided with a rapidity which appalled Baudelaire and which made him think that their quick agreement had been pre-arranged and instigated by some outside influence, that, while "Le Reniement de Saint Pierre" had in it an expression of violent disbelief as to the beneficent omnipotence of God, there was reasonable doubt to suppose that the author shared this feeling; but that the poems, "Les Bijoux," "Le Léthé," "A celle qui est trop gaie," "Lesbos," the first part of "Les Femmes damnées" and "Les métamorphoses du Vampire," certainly contained expressions of deliberate obscenity and must be eliminated from the book before it could be placed on public sale. Furthermore, the court in finding them guilty of deliberate "excitation of the senses by a realism gross and offensive to public morality," fined Baudelaire three hundred francs, Debroise and Poulet-Malassis, one hundred each, and costs of court.

Baudelaire left the court-room, sick with rage. When he was asked by Asselineau if he had expected acquittal, he cried, "Acquittal! I expected them to make a public vindication of my honor!" Debroise, in the company of Poulet-Malassis, who was trying to calm him, shook his fist in Baudelaire's face, accusing him of the ruin of his business and "the loss of his citizenship."

xxii

FOR A FEW DAYS, Baudelaire kept to his room, physically ill from rage and humiliation. He decided, however, that it would be better to appear with his head high in public, not to accept defeat, to pursue his cause and to continue his work. He decided, first of all, to appeal the case; but he was advised that, if he did not appeal the case, the fines would not have to be paid. With little heart in his work, he set about writing six new poems to take the place of those condemned, so that the book could be placed on sale again quickly.

He appeared as conspicuously as possible at the gathering places of the literati, defending himself vehemently. He was seen at Tortoni's with Marie Daubrun, the actress; at La Tour d'argent, at Cousinet's where the Goncourts remarked with disapproval his excessively cared for "woman's hands," his "loose, open shirt as if he were ready for the guillotine," and observed that he defended himself aloud and "in a cold rage." In his bitterness, he said that the French should be shown "a man's behind rather than his soul"; and argued that his judges and particularly his witless critics in the press seemed entirely incapable of understanding that every artist "as a perfect actor," must be able to make sensible, indeed, credible, "every sophism and every corruption." He decided that he would fight in every possible way to clear away this "enormous misunderstanding" which had cheated him of the glory and the fortune which were his "due."

Meantime, the attacks continued not only in the Parisian

press but in the provinces and Belgium as well. Asselineau had arranged finally to get his article into *La Revue française,* which managed to stem the flood a little and faintly affect public opinion. A woman who met Baudelaire socially at the time remarked, "I expected to meet a monster." Sainte-Beuve, avoiding a public consideration of the book in *Le Constitutionnel,* wrote Baudelaire a letter of thanks, saying that Baudelaire had created a new madness, had seemed to amuse himself "with the horrible," and, "without wishing to appear more prudish than I am," asked permission of Baudelaire to advise him "not to distrust passion so much," and "not to be afraid to be like everybody else." Hugo, pouting from Guernsey at the Second Empire, wrote Baudelaire that he "had just received, in the name of what it calls justice, one of the rare decorations which the present régime can accord. It is one more crown for you. I press your hand." A group of young people, including Léon Cladel, of no particular literary merit, who made their headquarters at the offices of Catulle Mendès at *La Revue fantaisiste* in the Passage Mirès, began imitating violently that outward phase of Baudelaire's work which was most misunderstood. But these doubtful manifestations did not comfort him for the attacks which continued and which were not only virulent but personal.

Henri Plassan in *La Gazette de Paris* had hoped that Baudelaire would be acquitted so that he could not assume a pose of fatality and be considered a martyr. Edouard Duranty in *Le Figaro* argued that Baudelaire's was a sick mind; that he had taken evil as his guide and that no one must be misled by "his veil of Catholicism." J. J. Weiss in *La Revue contemporaine* called Baudelaire's work "rubbish." In *Le Spectateur,* the moralist, Pontmartin, called it "an orgy." Habans in *Le Figaro* observed that "Monsieur Baudelaire finds eternity in the eyes of his cat; but that is nothing beside what he finds in the hair of his mistress." His old school friend, Louis Ménard, angry for the review Baudelaire had once written of his *Prométhée enchaînée,* now had opportunity for his revenge. Passing for an intimate of Baudelaire, Ménard wrote in *La Revue philosophique et religieuse,* "Monsieur Baudelaire wishes to pass himself off as a very wicked devil. His real trouble is that he lives in a fantastic world peopled with unhealthy shadows. Let him begin a normal life and he will be father of a family, will publish books he can read to his children. Until then, he will remain a school-boy, an arrested development."

xxiii

BAUDELAIRE FELT more than ever the need to clarify the intentions of his book, to win the recognition he had set out to gain. He continued working on the new poems and making an effort to write an explanatory preface for a second edition which he thought must follow quickly. He worked with his usual intensity and attention to detail; but the strain which the situation had put upon him, and his obligation to Michel Lévy for more translations of Poe, made him feel that it was difficult to do his best work. Furthermore, his creditors were upon him again all the more because his book had failed. His affairs could not have been worse and his nerves and health had suffered severely under the blow of the trial and conviction. In the cold silence of his hotel rooms, from long consideration of the injustice of his situation, he would pass into long periods of mental torpor from which he found it increasingly difficult to remove himself. Terrible neuralgic pains seemed to resist every treatment. And yet, with a terrific concentration, he continued to work. He declined invitations from friends and "a particularly charming" one from Richard Wagner.

But he had gone with Madame Sabatier to the theatre and had had several rendezvous with her in which she had tried to console him in the particular duress he was under. In an understandable moment, the consolation took a form of intimacy from which Baudelaire, sick in nerves, with his sensibilities at this moment particularly overwrought on this subject, immediately afterward recoiled. This was what he

hated most of all: to be deceived by the flesh. In an almost
brutal letter, with explanations which, Madame Sabatier
admitted, "a poor person of low intelligence" like herself
could not understand, he broke off relations with her. She
would not have it so. He wrote, insisting that they must not
take up where they left off. Jealous, Madame Sabatier replied
that she knew that "Jeanne's black face and black heart"
were between them. On Baudelaire's insistence, Madame
Sabatier, still not altogether comprehending, agreed to be
only "a friend."

Meantime, Baudelaire, eager for the warmth of "some
kind of home" where at least he would be relieved of the
necessity of "going out in snow and rain" for his meals and
would be spared the loneliness of hotel rooms, took up with
Jeanne again. She was ill now, a shadow of herself. Baudelaire now saw death where he had seen so much beauty; and
he felt that it was his responsibility that, in her condition,
she should not be a public care. With a great deal of difficulty, he had got an advance out of Ancelle, ransomed himself from his hotel room and furnished a small apartment.
He was scarcely installed, when, coming home one evening,
he found a Negro comfortably encamped with a pipe in
front of his fireplace. He turned out to be Jeanne's brother,
who had come from nowhere at all to live out on Baudelaire
a debt which Jeanne had incurred with him. To make matters worse, he had no respect whatever for Baudelaire's
privacy. Baudelaire could not tolerate this long, and, with a
promise never to let Jeanne want while he could earn a sou,
he made a definite break with her and accepted his mother's
invitation to come to live with her at Honfleur.

xxiv

MONSIEUR EMON, the general's former aide-de-camp, and Madame Aupick's neighbor at Honfleur had settled her estate for her. It was discovered that, in spite of the General's success in military, diplomatic and political life, his fortune was not so munificent as it might have been. The income from his estate was so small that Madame Aupick had petitioned for a pension which she obtained with the collaboration of Monsieur Fould, Minister of State, who had not found it expedient to aid Baudelaire in his extremity. It was a pension of five thousand francs. With this and with the proceeds of the sale of horses, carriages and equipment from the town house, Madame Aupick settled in the cottage at Honfleur, which the General had bought as a pied-à-terre in which to spend the hot months. It was in an elevated section of the town on the Rue Neubourg. It had a garden which was Madame Aupick's chief occupation. In the rear of the garden was a little kiosque from which one could see Havre, Harfleur and the sea. She had as neighbors Monsieur Emon and his family and other families who had long been intimates of the Aupicks.

Although Baudelaire had been eager to go to his mother upon the death of the General, it was not only the continued presence of these neighbors which had kept him away, but also the demands on him in the preparation of *Les Fleurs du mal* and the exigencies of the trial. Furthermore, in the correspondence which Baudelaire kept up constantly with his mother, sometimes writing as many as four or five letters a day to her, in the midst of the usual recriminations, protestations of affection and intense solicitude for her health, demands for money, he kept telling her that he did not wish to see her unless he had something good to tell her. He was thinking, of course, of the ultimate success of his book.

The book had failed; but he did not believe that the book was a failure. While his health and spirit had been badly shaken, he had not lost confidence in his greatness. And, while it was a considerable shock to his pride to have to return to his mother, to whom he had been trying to prove for the last fifteen years that he had talent, not only still under almost unanimous attack by the press, but also with the echoes of the court trial a juicy bit of scandal for all Paris and a great part of the provinces, he felt that he must nevertheless take advantage of this invitation.

Paris had become hateful to him. For all his effort to resist, to clarify "the great misunderstanding," he felt that he must get away somewhere to find peace, to recuperate his forces, to settle his mind, finish his new preface, finish work in hand, and begin some new work which would at least support his new effort with *Les Fleurs du mal*. Moreover, in his room at the Hôtel de Dieppe which was next to the Gare de l'Ouest, he could no longer bear the racket of Monsieur Guizot's beloved trains. Every noise "struck him in the stomach." He was already beginning to have those moments when, for no apparent reason, he would fall.

Furthermore, his mother had been insistent with her invitations, more especially since his trouble in Paris. She was overwhelmed by the attacks. She had been especially horrified by that of J. J. Weiss in *La Revue contemporaine*. Baudelaire had not spared her any of the details of these attacks, sending her clippings of all of them, even of Bourdin's, saying in connection with this last, "When you see your son thus mistreated, do not laugh!" Madame Aupick knew that her son was suffering.

She therefore insisted upon his coming, saying that as for the neighbors they came infrequently and he need not meet them, if he wished. She told him that she had prepared a room for him. He wrote back eagerly, asking if he could have a view of the sea from it. She had, indeed, prepared him an excellent room, large, as he liked it; and it over-looked the garden, the superb sand dunes and the sea. She set about having it renovated and painted. He inquired with some perturbation whether the walls were damp from the sea; for he had a little collection of paintings, largely gifts and small items he had picked up cheaply, of Courbet, Jongkind and later of Manet, to say nothing of his father's portrait, with which he wished to decorate his room. While his mother had finished arrangements for his coming early in 1858, it was not until almost the beginning of the next year that he arrived.

XXV

HE WAS DETAINED in Paris by financial and literary matters. In the first place, he had not only saddled himself with another obligation to the amount of three thousand francs which he had taken in advances from Poulet-Malassis and of which he could guarantee payment only by making out his will in favor of his publisher; but his usual debt situation had become so acute that he had to stay in hiding for several days to save himself from arrest. Then, for his current expenses he had to waste time running out to Neuilly to beg money from Ancelle who required a long conversation on art, politics and religion, before he would come to the point. Furthermore, after Baudelaire's conviction by the court, Ancelle would waste more of Baudelaire's time by coming frequently to Paris "to assassinate" him, as Baudelaire put it, with offers of assistance. Baudelaire used to have to walk back and forth for hours in front of his hotel, hesitating to go for fear of meeting baliffs or of finding Ancelle installed in his room, prepared to make him lose hours of work.

For he was now, in spite of everything, working assiduously. Almost immediately after his trial, a new little review, *Le Présent,* which had already printed two poems, "Hymne," one of the Sabatier cycle, and "La Rançon," a promise to show God on "that terrible day," "a grange full of harvest and of flowers," had accepted five prose-poems, a new medium in which he was experimenting. He was delighted to be so quickly presented to the public again. Four of these pieces, "La Chevelure," "L'Horloge," "L'Invitation au voyage" and "Crepuscule du soir" were really the dessous, the material of poems of the same name some of which had already appeared in *Les Fleurs du mal,* but which were here presented in a cadenced prose admittedly inspired by *Gaspard de la nuit* but with a sharpness of image and effect entirely new to French literature. The other two were "Les Projets" and "Solitude." The first celebrated the making of plans as being much more pleasant and profitable than carrying them out; and the second paraphrased Pascal's sentiment that one's greatest misfortunes spring from not having known enough to remain at home.

While no particular comment reached him with respect to these, a little praise came to him for his paper in *L'Artiste* on Flaubert on the occasion of a new edition of *Madame Bovary,* and for his study of caricaturists, which appeared in *Le Présent.* The study on Flaubert was notable for its attack on a world "which has definitely abjured the love of the spirit and which, neglecting the great sentiments of antiquity, has interest only in its belly." In the paper on caricaturists, with his usual excellent judgment in art, he went straight to Daumier as superior to Pigal, Charlet and even to Monnier and Gavarni.

La Revue contemporaine had taken his "De l'idéal de l'artifice," which served later as a sort of introduction to *Les Paradis artificiels.* Furthermore, his desk was piled with uncorrected proofs of his translation, *Les Aventures d'Arthur Gordon Pym.* Michel Lévy was writing him "insolent letters" about them, and, once again, he found himself "nailed at Corbeil," fussing with type-setters and offering to pay for destroyed forms. *Les Aventures d'Arthur Gordon Pym* appeared without any comment from the press.

Then there was the matter of an unexpurgated edition of *Les Fleurs du mal* which Pincebourde, Poulet-Malassis' chief clerk was offering to bring out in Belgium, but which Baude-laire would not agree to for fear it would hurt the future sales of Poulet-Malassis.

When, finally, his affairs were passably settled, along with the business of packing his books and his "paperasses" which he supervised nervously and which he sent off with great trepidation from Paris, with great warnings to his mother not to let anyone touch them, he arrived in Honfleur late in the winter of 1858.

xxvi

IN SPITE OF THE SEASON, the weather was mild; and he was at once delighted with the aspect and situation of the house, which he immediately christened "La Maison Joujou." There was the sun, as he always had written of it, "shining upon the sea"; and, above, "those magnificent and changing cities which the clouds make." And close by, too, lived Boudin, on the Rue de l'Homme de Bois, whom Corot had called "the king of cloud painters" and who had come especially to paint the cloud effects over the sea, noted to be especially beautiful at Honfleur. Baudelaire spent time frequently with him among the chalk cliffs; but he declined to leave cards at the Emon's or at any of the houses of former friends of the General. He had a further grudge against Monsieur Emon because it was to him his mother had gone for an opinion on *Les Fleurs du mal.*

Baudelaire was considerably irritated by his mother's insisting upon setting a place at the table for the General at every meal. His mother, too, thought that now was the opportunity to try to reform Baudelaire; to get him somehow to straighten out his life. Bailiffs had managed even to reach Honfleur. There were acrimonious tiffs with his mother on this subject, always ending in the assertion of Baudelaire that, with the steady work he would now be able to engage in, he was certain to succeed. Furthermore, he used to plead with her that since there were now only the two of them, not counting that cretin of a half-brother who was a comfortable magistrate at Fontainbleau, it would be better for them to try to find as much comfort as possible in each other.

After rushing back to Paris for one day in order to dispose of the furniture in the apartment he had occupied with Jeanne and to see that she was comfortably installed in a modest maison de santé in the Faubourg Saint-Denis, he came back to Honfleur with the resolution to remain there as long as possible.

Baudelaire was certain that Honfleur would restore him in every possible way. He was glad to get away from Paris. He adopted Honfleur as his own at once. He strolled about the town, making himself important at the post-office with his mass of mail and his great packages of proofs. Barbey d'Aurevilly kept him posted on his escapades with his blonde Englishwoman and informed him in one letter that the poetic rage in Paris was that "wind-bag," Mistral. Baudelaire would stop at the pharmacist's where he would discuss the effects of opium and hashish, a somewhat extended treatment of which he was incorporating in his *Paradis artificiels*. He became a familiar figure, in his top hat and flowing coat, at the café where the waiters attended respectfully to his needs and indulged with him in bits of town gossip. A tremendous scandal swept the town while he was there. The wife of a local dignitary had been caught in a reprehensible attitude with a town councillor in a confessional of the town church. In a letter to Barbey d'Aurevilly, Baudelaire had a good laugh over the incident, saying that it brought back all the heart-warming stimulus of "les vieilles saloperies françaises," that it had all the flavor of an incident right out of Restif de la Bretonne.

In the quiet of his large, cheerful room, full of sun and air, with his papers, pictures and books about him, with the town, the estuary of the Seine and the ocean visible from his window, he felt that here was the place to gather his forces to win what he wished to win from the world.

At the beginning, there was an incident which unsettled

him considerably for a while. He had given the Abbé Cardenne, curé of the town church, a copy of *Les Fleurs du mal*. The priest had requested Baudelaire to let him see it. Baudelaire had had some walks with the priest by the sea and through the town and had written to Poulet-Malassis that he was "erudite, almost remarkable." Some days later, Baudelaire had asked the Abbé for his opinion of the book. The Abbé had answered coldly that he had burned it in his fireplace. Baudelaire raged; and, after that, "every time," as he told Asselineau, "that I would decide to make a definite step in the direction of he church, I would think of the Abbé Cardenne."

Nevertheless, Baudelaire had here the most tranquil and perhaps the most productive time of his life. He worked steadily in his room, too steadily, sometimes, for his mother's taste; she would have preferred him to be out of doors rather than agonizing over things which she considered much less important than his health. In the six months that he passed at Honfleur, he not only finished the six poems to take the place of those condemned, but twenty-six more, among them the magnificent "Voyage," "Hymne à la beauté" and "Obsession." He added substantially to the collection of prose-poems which he hoped to bring out later in a volume.

La Revue contemporaine published the poems "Les petites vieilles," and "Les sept vieillards," which, because of their humanitarian nature, he dedicated to Victor Hugo. Hugo responded with a letter thanking Baudelaire and saying, "You say Art for Art; I Art for Progress, which amounts to the same thing. You have created a new thrill. Persecutions! Courage! Greatness!" The letter irritated Baudelaire; but because of Hugo's name, he asked for permission to use it as a preface to his study of Gautier which *L'Artiste* had brought out and which Poulet-Malassis was going to publish as a brochure. For purely financial reasons and without success, he tried to finish his play, *Le Marquis du Premier Housards*.

He completed *Les Paradis artificiels* and his "Salon de 1859." This latter which appeared, in part, in *La Revue française,* was perhaps, the most profound and most technical of his "Salons." Perhaps for this reason, it did not attract as much public notice as the others. In it, Baudelaire attacked progressivism again, was transfixed before the superb *La Mise au Tombeau* and *Le Saint Sébastien* of Delacroix; and brought to the attention of the French public the etchings of Charles Méryon whose "majesties of stone, belfries, obelisks of industry, prodigious scaffoldings on monuments in process of repair and tumultuous skies," drew him much more than those roomfuls of "excellently finished platitudes."

But with these finished, Baudelaire found himself eager to return to Paris in order to press his interests. A visit by Courbet to Honfleur suddenly determined Baudelaire to return with him. He made this decision against his mother's plea that he stay on at Honfleur and continue his work from there. He hastily gathered some things together and took the train with Courbet.

xxvii

HE ARRIVED IN Paris in the midst of a newspaper squabble about him, started by Hippolyte Babou in *La Revue française*. Babou wrote, in an article entitled "Concerning Literary Friendships," that Sainte-Beuve had deliberately remained silent during the trial, when a word from him would perhaps have saved Baudelaire. Sainte-Beuve answered indignantly in an article in *Le Constitutionnel* that he had written a letter at the time to Baudelaire, giving him considerable advice and that he thought his "young friend" "one of the most important props of the Romantic decadence." In a kind of terror, Baudelaire wrote at once to Sainte-Beuve, disclaiming any connection with Babou's article and calling it irresponsible and "a school-boy's prank." He wrote Babou, begging him not to do any more to alienate him from "this powerful and dangerous old man." Baudelaire then began to woo Sainte-Beuve with letters flattering some of his reviews and with gifts of English gingerbread which he knew that Sainte-Beuve liked. He wrote many notes, making appointments on any or no pretext to see Sainte-Beuve, but always managed to find him busy or "out."

Meantime, Baudelaire, in addition to his constant work on a new volume of Poe, and the preparation of the "second first edition" of *Les Fleurs du mal,* was occupied with the printing of *Les Paradis artificiels* which Poulet-Malassis, under the somewhat disapproving eye of Debroise, had agreed to publish. In the beginning, Baudelaire had a considerable row with Poulet-Malassis, who wished to include in the book an advertisement of a pharmacist! Baudelaire, who had tried hashish at the Hôtel Pimodan, had long played with the idea of writing something of the effects of stimulants and drugs on the human will and intelligence. He had been a great deal moved by the life of De Quincey and by the "Confessions of an Opium Eater," parts of which he incorporated in his own work. He begins by dedicating the book to a woman who had often beheld him "in Orestes-like sleep" and "with a light and maternal hand" had dispersed the frightful dream, and who now had her own eyes "upon heaven, that place of all the transfigurations." In this book he expresses again his preference for the Infinite. He discusses the world of the spirit, and the natural world—for which latter he had "so little taste that, in the same way that they say idle and sensitive women write their confidences to imaginary friends," he "would willingly write only for the dead." He points out that man, who is born with the desire for the Infinite, tries to get it by the quick route, by some compromise, by some formula from the pharmacist's, by which he can have his body on earth and his soul in paradise. He does not understand that "if he does not accept the conditions of life, he sells his soul"; that he "is militating against the intentions of God," who demands the purifying work of time.

This book, on the whole, was better received than *Les Fleurs du mal*. He was somewhat flattered by an article by Dalloz which said that the book "could have been written by Sainte-Beuve." Albert Glatigny wrote a highly appreciative review for *L'Orphéon*. Claudin, of *Le Moniteur,* called it excellent. Barbey d'Aurevilly, in *Le Pays,* at first upset Baudelaire with his precarious word-juggling—he had to say: "This is the hell of Monsieur Baudelaire. He is Satan here as he was Heliogabalus in *Les Fleurs du mal*," before ultimately praising the work. Lescure, in *La Gazette de*

France, called Baudelaire "a militant puritan, a preacher, a soldier of the spirit." Although the government for some time hesitated to license the book, Baudelaire felt that with it he was making up for some of the ground lost on the appearance of the first *Fleurs du mal,* and would prepare the public better for the second which was to be printed soon.

An American by the name of Stoepel, after asking nearly everyone else of literary importance in Paris, finally requested Baudelaire to translate Longfellow's "Pipe of Peace" into French. It was Stoepel's purpose to set this to music and to present it at La Salle Pasdeloup. Baudelaire was impressed with the American's talk of publicity and prospects of a large sale of tickets. He worked hard to complete the translation for Stoepel; but Stoepel, shortly afterward, slipped away without paying for the translation, without giving the programme or making any explanation to Baudelaire.

It was about this time, too, that Baudelaire had a violent break with De Calonne, editor of *La Revue contemporaine,* who had taken a group of Baudelaire's poems, among them, notably, the magnificent "Voyage." This poem De Calonne declared "weak" and notified Baudelaire that he intended to make changes. Baudelaire stormed into the offices of *La Revue contemporaine,* threatening to beat De Calonne if he touched a line. Baudelaire was, however, helpless in this situation because De Calonne had already advanced money to him and refused to return the poems on his demand. After many violent exchanges, Baudelaire settled the matter to his satisfaction, but lost the good will of De Calonne.

La Revue fantaisiste accepted studies by Baudelaire of nine of his contemporaries. Aside from the single review of Louis Ménard's *Prométhée enchaîné,* some fifteen years before, the article on Flaubert and the brochure on Théophile Gautier, these were the first important efforts of Baudelaire at literary criticism. These gave him the opportunity to elaborate his views on literature and to inform the public, indirectly, of what he was trying to do in his own work. The studies were somewhat limited in critical candor because they dealt, for the most part, with people who were his friends or whose support he desired. He treated kindly the devoted Asselineau's *La Double Vie* and had only the best to say for Barbey d'Aurevilly and Théodore de Banville whom he praised for being able to make beauty and peace out of "ugliness and stupidity." He is extremely courteous to the "feminine sincerity" of Marceline-Desbordes Valmore. He speaks of the "triumphant poetry" of his friend Leconte de Lisle, which has "no other purpose but itself." His praise of Hugo, while apparently excessive, has suggestions of a reserved judgment. He says, for example, that Hugo is not moral purposely but "through the superabundance of his nature." He is "a colossus with a tear in his eye; and that is something of an originality." To Pétrus Borel, he gives his proper place as one of the stars in "the sombre Romantic sky." Auguste Barbier he gently chides for spoiling "superb poetic faculties with a false idea of poetry."

It is rather in asides springing from the personalities under discussion that Baudelaire expresses something of his own literary attitude and intentions. He tries to explain the confessional attitude by saying that "the modern artist has a tendency to take pleasure in explaining himself." By implication, he admits that his use of irony is "the vengeance of the vanquished." And, so much out of gear with his time, so anxious for the Absolute, so confused yet as to how to reach it, he declares that "the mystery has discouraged thought. In spite of Newton and Laplace, the scientific attitude does not exist. Matter, movement, multiplicity are merely the breathing and the aspiration of Deity whose unique function is to give forth universes and call them in."

xxviii

THE SECOND EDITION of *Les Fleurs du mal* was nearly ready. He was depending upon a wide circulation to bring him the recognition he thought his due. He was having trouble with the frontispiece. He wished a skeleton "arborescent with arms outstretched so as to form a Cross"; and Poulet-Malassis had suggested Bracquemond to do it. Baudelaire was not satisfied with the result. He thought that Gustave Doré, with his genius for Romantic clouds, backgrounds and fantastic vegetation, could have done better. He decided to try to find Rethel's *Danse Macabre,* which he had once seen, and perhaps use that. It was ultimately decided to use neither. He thought again of the necessity of some sort of explanatory preface and wrote, in part, that "this book, essentially useless and absolutely innocent, was made for no other reason than to amuse myself and exercise my passionate taste for overcoming obstacles," but finally gave up the idea.

The thirty-six new poems, which were added to the second edition, were all done with Baudelaire's intense preoccupation for perfection. As with the first edition, he had left nothing to accident, feeling that "inspiration is the result of constant revision." Finally the book appeared in February, 1861. Among the new poems were notably "Hymne à la beaute," "Le Voyage," "Obsession" and "Le Rêve d'un curieux." They reiterated his hope that the achievement of beauty might open for him the door of the Infinite:

> Comme tu me plairais, O Nuit! sans ces étoiles
> Dont la lumière parle un langage connu!
> Car je cherche le vide, et le noir; [1]

They repeated his weariness and horror of the natural world
where he sees:

> Du haut jusques en bas de l'échelle fatale,
> Le spectacle ennuyeux de l'immortel péché. . . . [2]

and, in general, his desire to achieve the ideal.

The response in the press was not so immediate or over-
whelming as it had been in the case of the first edition.
People with whom he had arranged for reviews, responded,
of course, first. *La Revue anecdotique,* which was published
as an advertising medium by Poulet-Malassis, declared the
book "a literary event." No other passably favorable account
appeared until nearly a year later when Leconte de Lisle
wrote, in *La Revue européenne,* that Baudelaire was gifted
with "tact, originality, energy"; and that "he must be par-
doned many things because he loves exclusively the beautiful." The adverse notices were almost as leisurely. In *La
Revue brittanique,* Amédée Pichot wrote that the book was
"not bad," but not nearly so good as the work of Auguste
Lacaussade. *Le Figaro* acknowledged that Baudelaire was an
artist of intelligence but believed that he suffered from poor
choice of subjects. Charles Valette declared in *La Causerie*
that Baudelaire had a "good style," but "if you want to read
a great poet, read Hugo." Alphonse Duchesne, in *Le Figaro,*

---

[1] How you would please me, O Night, without those stars
   Whose light speaks a known language!
   For I seek emptiness and darkness! . . .
            "Obsession."
[2] From top to bottom of the fatal scale
   The weary spectacle of immortal sin. . . .
            "Le Voyage."

observed that the poems were an "impure mixture of pagan corruption." Ponmartin inquired, in *La Revue des Deux-Mondes,* "What kind of society could there be which would accept Baudelaire as its poet?" Moret, in *La Causerie,* declared that "never did a more violent man sing more empty things in a more impossible tongue." And *Le Boulevard* published a caricature of Baudelaire falling out of bed in an extremely disordered room peopled by demons and ghosts, entitling it, "A Night of Monsieur Baudelaire." Baudelaire was only mildly comforted by reading in the London *Spectator* an article by an unknown person named Swinburne, which said that, "after Hugo," he was perhaps the greatest poet of his time.

But Baudelaire made further friendships at this time which, to some degree, flattered him. Léon Cladel, who was among the first of the young men to call him "Master," dedicated his first book, *Les Amours éternels,* to Baudelaire. Another young man by the name of Villiers de L'Isle-Adam, with nine hundred years of Catholicism and noble lineage behind him, moved by every aspect of Baudelaire's poetry, sought him out. Next to Catulle Mendès, Baudelaire found him the most interesting of the younger writers. Villiers had composed music for Baudelaire's "Le Vin" and had sung it himself at La Salle Pasdeloup. Villier's world attitude pleased Baudelaire because it was largely like his own. Villiers was already contemplating a study of scientism, a study of the dubious spiritual value of material progress, which was to become the substance of his book on Edison called *L'Ève future.* He was associated with Catholic Action, and brought to Baudelaire's attention a life of Christ by a man named Sepp and some works of the monk, Dom Guéranger. Villiers discussed with Baudelaire mysticism, the terror of annihilation which ultimately, in the words of Villiers, "brings one to one's knees." These were the talks which brought Baudelaire closer to the idea of a return to the Church. But his great passion was still his reputation.

Charles Méryon also sought out Baudelaire. He came to thank Baudelaire for his kind mention of his etchings in the "Salon de 1859." Baudelaire not only admired Méryon's magnificent etchings of Paris, but he pitied him profoundly. Méryon had been a captain in the French Navy. He discovered suddenly that he could draw; and he had suffered so deeply when his work did not receive recognition and money that his mind became affected. He had already spent some time at Charenton when Baudelaire met him. Baudelaire made every effort to assist him, nagging the Ministry of Beaux-Arts into buying a set of these etchings of "historical importance," and trying to induce Poulet-Malassis, Delâtre and other publishers to bring them out. He offered to write a short poem to illustrate each etching; but, on Méryon's second and last visit to Baudelaire, tall, dark, heavily bearded and hollow-eyed, "he stood, with his hat in his hand, looking at the ceiling," as Baudelaire talked, and flatly declined Baudelaire's offer, preferring to write his own poems. Baudelaire answered that this did not matter; that he would help him to the utmost in any case and thought that the interview was ended. But Méryon did not go. He still stood looking at the ceiling. Suddenly, he pointed out to Baudelaire on one of the etchings of Paris which he had brought, that the deep shadows on one of the stone walls was a perfect profile of a sphynx. The sphynx, declared Méryon, indicated the Emperor, and the birds, which he had drawn in the sky, were eagles presaging evil for Louis Napoleon.

Then, just as suddenly, he asked Baudelaire if he had ever read any of the work of Edgar Allan Poe. To Baudelaire's statement that it was he who was responsible for Poe being read at all in France, Méryon replied that Poe had not written his work at all, but "a clever group of men." Then he added, "Take 'The Murders in the Rue Morgue,' I have made a drawing of that Morgue. There is an ourang-outang involved. This monkey murders two women, a mother and a daughter. I, also, have morally assassinated two women, a mother and her daughter. I have always taken the story as an allusion to my misfortunes." He then asked Baudelaire if he would do him the favor of finding the date "when Edgar Poe, supposing that he was not helped by anyone, composed the story, so that I can see if the date coincides with that of my adventure."

After that, while continuing to work for his interests, Baudelaire declined to see Méryon any more. Baudelaire was frequently upset to find under his door a note like the one reading, "I called, hoping to find from your own lips that you were not angry with me; for I do not think I could have done anything to you which would serve as a motive for your change in manner"; or else, "my last letter has remained unanswered. I have left my name at your dwelling many times without the slightest word from you. I am entitled to know why you have broken relations with me." Baudelaire made no further effort to get in touch with Méryon, but wrote Asselineau that he could not bear to see Méryon; for, each time that he had seen him, he had asked himself how it happened that "I, who have everything in my mind and nerves to drive me mad, have not become so yet."

Baudelaire had been invited to Wagner's famous Wednesdays supervised, in the Rue Newton, by the charming Minna, and made casual and intimate by the presence of Wagner's dog, Fips. Berlioz and Gounod attended these afternoons also; and while they were somewhat stiff with Baudelaire whom they considered something of an outsider, they gave him the opportunity to hear and talk music. Baudelaire had early become a Wagnerite, attending assiduously the first concerts at La Salle Pasdeloup. He, with Léon Leroy, the Gaspérinis and Champfleury, was among the first to defend Wagner against the attacks of "imbecile critics" and "the brutish French public."

In 1861, on the occasion of Wagner's presentation at the Opera of his *Tannhäuser,* Baudelaire was so disgusted by the howls and mock applause which the work received, and by the personal insult which Madame Wagner had had to accept from a critic as she left the Opera, that he determined to rebuke the French and defend Wagner in an article.

In the offices of *La Revue européenne,* which had agreed to publish the article, Baudelaire sat down at ten in the morning and, working without interruption until ten that night finished the paper which he called *Richard Wagner et Tannhäuser.* After asking the French, in respect to the frightful scandal at the Opera, "What will Europe think of us?" he tells them that he will not allow this impression to get abroad without some effort on his part to bring home to the French the beauty and importance of the work they had tried to destroy. Personally, he says that he "was lifted from the earth" by the majesty and intention of the music. He felt, by the "correspondence of color, sound and idea, absolute solitude, a solitude of immense horizons." He comprehended "fully the idea of a soul moving in light . . . beyond nature." He was tremendously impressed by Wagner's magnificent projection of the idea of the conflict between Satan and God, in which "the intimate sense of God" is at first overwhelmed by the concupiscences of the flesh; and then, "as the music of the religious theme, invading evil, little by little, establishes order, takes the ascendant; as in all its solid beauty, it rises above the chaos of agonizing voluptuousness, the soul feels . . . a kind of salvation." Baudelaire expresses his own spiritual effort and his own desire without allowing himself to advance to the fulfillment intimated in the Opera. He had still his world to conquer.

On the whole, the article was well received. Dentu hastened to publish it as a brochure. Catulle Mendès, of course, wrote a very favorable notice of the brochure in *La Revue fantaisiste*. Valette praised Baudelaire in *La Causerie* "for defending Wagner against a public which would not let a masterpiece be born." Wagner wrote Baudelaire a letter saying that the article had encouraged him "more than anything said about my poor talent," and wondered how any "French writer could know so much." Charles Bataille, in *La Revue fantaisiste,* wondered whether it wasn't too soon to cry, "genius!" Albert de Fizelière in *Le Boulevard* asked bluntly, in substance, "What does Baudelaire know about it?"

xxix

AT THIS TIME, Baudelaire made a bold, and, to his friends and enemies alike, an incomprehensible step. He announced himself a candidate for election to the French Academy. The uproar which followed this announcement in Arsène Houssaye's *La Presse,* was tremendous. Two chairs were vacant, the Lacordaire, and, upon his recent death, the Eugène Scribe. Flaubert was astounded that Baudelaire wanted to sit among the Academicians. It was known that, with the possible exception of Alfred de Vigny, Baudelaire considered them, Victor Hugo included, as "wind heads" and "old fools." Flaubert promised Baudelaire, in any case, that he would ask Jules Sandeau to support him. Baudelaire assured Flaubert that if he did not receive a single vote, he would not repent. In a letter to his mother, he had declared that he had proposed his name to the secretary, Villemain, "on the advice of several friends"; that, while, for himself, he "did not need the approval of these numb-skulls," he knew that she "loved public honors." Furthermore, there was "a small emolument" attached to this honor which, after all, was the "only one which a true literary man could solicit without blushing." He asked her to write a note for him to the Academician Lebrun, but to let him see it before she sent it. Baudelaire had written to Arsène Houssaye at the time he sent the announcement to *La Presse,* saying that Houssaye could publish his declaration "without danger"; for he was "personally without hope"; and that, even though "he had enough trouble," he was offering himself as a candidate "for the pleasure of becoming the goat for all unfortunate men of letters." The reason, as Asselineau has it, was that Baudelaire desired " a public affirmation of his talent."

Seventeen men, the most deserving of whom, according to Baudelaire, was Octave Feuillet, presented themselves as candidates. Gautier did not present himself because he "did not wish to compromise his dignity." Baudelaire set to work immediately campaigning for the chair, sending out copies of his books and making the personal visits, which are de rigueur, "on foot and in rags." He "did not have the courage to approach Thiers and Guizot." In addition to requesting a letter from Flaubert to Sandeau, he asked Asselineau to get him introductions to Ponsard and Augier.

After cooling his heels for a long time in the outer offices of *Le Constitutionnel,* he managed to see Sainte-Beuve. Sainte-Beuve said to him, "I knew your boldness but this overwhelms me"; but "since the harm was already done," he would write an article for him in the newspaper. And, indeed, Sainte-Beuve wrote in *Le Constitutionnel* a criticism of the electoral methods of the Academy and added that Baudelaire's announcement of himself as candidate was not a hoax, a trick of some sort, but was serious and "possibly a means of promoting the candidacy of his master, Théophile Gautier." In any case, Sainte-Beuve continued, "Monsieur Baudelaire deserves to be heard." He declared that Baudelaire was polite, "a nice boy," who, "at the extremes of language, has built himself a kiosque where one reads Poe and takes hashish, opium and abominable drugs of all sorts in little cups of exquisite china." He called this "kiosque," "the Kamtchatka, the madness of Baudelaire."

Maxime du Camp told Baudelaire that this article was a public insult. And, indeed, although Baudelaire had never before expressed chagrin at Sainte-Beuve's consistent refusal to review his books and was even, after this, to stand respectful attendance upon him, to be overwhelmed with sincere solicitude for the great man's health when he was temporarily immobilized by "a congestion," and was (albeit with a somewhat ironic reserve), to congratulate his "dear uncle" upon his ultimate elevation as Senator of the Empire, he was deeply hurt by this article. He wrote Sainte-Beuve: "Thank you for what you call 'my Kamtchatka.' I compliment the journalist. One thing struck me that here I find all the good sense and petulance of your conversation. I should have liked to collaborate. I would have been able to furnish you two or three enormities which you overlooked."

This temporary huff did not prevent Baudelaire from going back to Sainte-Beuve for more advice concerning his candidacy. Upon Sainte-Beuve's insistence that he should give up trying for the chair, Baudelaire stunned him by declaring that, after all, he was, perhaps, wrong in applying for the Scribe chair; that, since there was scarcely any resemblance between him and Scribe, he would apply for the chair of Lacordaire; for, between himself and "that Romantic priest," there was certainly a "resemblance of language and Christian sentiment." He stated that he would consider writing a paper on Lacordaire and passing it around to members of the Academy.

Meantime, with the press hammering in his ears that the Academy was "no place for an Anti-Christ," he began his visits among the members. He wrote to his mother that, despite the commotion, his chances were not so bad, since he had as his most formidable opponent only "that ridiculous Prince de Broglie, son of the Duc de Broglie, already a member." He wrote to Sainte-Beuve that he thought that the real men of letters would vote for him and that he was at least "as much of a Christian as Villemain." Patin, against whom everybody had warned him, had been charming, but feared that Baudelaire "had reached him too late." De Sacy had been extremely courteous. Alfred de Vigny, an old man dying in his apartments in the Rue des Écuries-Artois, while advising Baudelaire to withdraw, had talked amiably with him for three hours on art and literature.

Viennet had lectured Baudelaire on poetry, saying, "My dear Monsieur Baudelaire, there are five classes of poetry: tragic, comic, epic, satiric and occasional poetry which includes the fable in which I excel." Villemain, beginning by receiving Baudelaire with a contemptuousness which Baudelaire swore he "would some day make him pay for," at once attacked "the toxicology which was the morality of *Les Paradis artificiels*," and then Baudelaire's "originality," saying that he hated originality and that he himself was "not original." It was these interviews that made Baudelaire remark to De Vigny that a satire should be written on the whole business of Academic elections. Lamartine, courteous on the surface, in asking him to withdraw, had, as Baudelaire afterward wrote to his mother, "paid me a compliment so monstrous that I cannot repeat it. He is, after all, a man of the world, that is to say, a kind of whore."

On the first ballot, Baudelaire received no votes. The Prince de Broglie was elected.

This was the slap in the face which he expected and yet had not expected. One of his friends suggested that perhaps he had an exaggerated impression of his genius. He was somewhat relieved to know that the Academy had been pleased with "the tone and tact" of his letter of withdrawal, written when he saw that he had received no votes on the first ballot. Friends, like Flaubert, tried to console him by asking him why he bothered in the first place. Little reviews, like *L'Indépendance*, which had heretofore been his partisans, called him "not a benefactor to unfortunate men of letters" but "a traitor" to the cause of independent writing. Upon seeing his mother soon after this, he went into a sort of rage, saying that "as soon as he made his fortune," he would write a book showing up "the fraudulent culture of the French." To Flaubert, to whom he had written that his effort to be elected was a "brain-storm out of which he was trying to make wisdom," he admitted that the whole business was a catastrophe; but to Asselineau and Poulet-Malassis, he kept insisting that he had presented himself to the Academy, to see whether the Academicians, as he suspected, would prefer to a man of talent, without considerable political attachments, anybody even "their janitors, provided they were Orleanists."

XXX

IN "LE JOUEUR GÉNÉREUX," one of the twenty poems in prose with the title *Spleen de Paris,* which *La Presse* had accepted and for which Baudelaire was paid a thousand francs, the best pay he had ever received for shorter contributions, he expressed the mild satanism he was then trying to sustain. "In gambling," he wrote, "I lost my soul—often such an impalpable, useless, indeed, troublesome thing that, in its loss, I felt rather less emotion than if I had mislaid a visiting-card." In "Le Chien et le flacon," of the same group, there was a burst of bitterness: "One must offer only carefully selected garbage to the public." In another, he sees in a "painfully cravatted Frenchman" wishing a Happy New Year to a donkey in the streets of Paris, "the spirit of France." Here too, in these carefully worked efforts at vivid and cogent observations "of the modern world," inspired by the method of Aloysius Bertrand but so superior to him, he returns to his hatred of the masses, saying "Perhaps we must beat men to make them worthy, proud and understanding." And yet, in these poems, as already recently in "Les petites vieilles" and "Les sept vieillards," he resumes momentarily, a humanitarianism which he had not expressed so fully since 1848. He cannot bear "the eyes of the poor," the "reflection of the joys of the rich in the eyes of the poor." He cannot bear the sight of "abandoned old women." And he can find no peace. His nerves, painfully "tense and loud," are upset by "the selfish turbulence of children." In the passion of his disappointment, he thinks of God, but not yet as a refuge.

He seeks solitude in the "chastity of the sea," in the "drugs
of the intelligence." He wishes to find some woman in the
"autumn of her life," "full of servile tenderness." And these
failing, he turns to the outlet of deliberate perversity as in
"Le Mauvais Vitrier," wishing to destroy through "a peri-
lous but refreshing impulsion"; or, as in "Mademoiselle
Bistouri," always seeking "to unveil the mystery" and always
sensible of "the horror that God had planted" in his heart
in order "to convert him," when faced with horror in the
person of Mademoiselle Bistouri, who prefers doctors as
lovers, who wants them to come to her in "their gowns and
aprons with still a little blood upon them," he cries, "Lord,
God, you the Sovereign who permits us to do as we like,
have pity upon the mad!"

xxxi

EDOUARD MANET had sought out Baudelaire. Bringing to
Paris from Holland a wife combining so many qualities of
beauty and intelligence that Baudelaire feared that "she
must be a monster," Manet opened a studio to which he
invited Baudelaire. Baudelaire shared the Manets' preference
for the music of Liszt and Wagner; and he was a frequent
visitor at their Thursday musicales. Here he met Fantin-
Latour who included a fine head of Baudelaire in his great
painting, *Hommage à Delacroix,* made upon the occasion of
Delacroix's death. Here too, he met Monsieur and Madame
Paul Meurice, who while they always had his interest at
heart, did not particularly impress Baudelaire. Monsieur
Meurice antagonized him with his inclination to the mate-
rialist principles of the day. And Madame Meurice annoyed
him somewhat by the excessive effort she made to appear
interested in the arts and to attack the things which she
imagined he considered worthy of attack. But, on the whole,
Baudelaire enjoyed these people.

He had, moreover, recognized at once in Manet, "a bold
man capable of creating something new." In a poem, he
called Manet's *Lola de Valence* "a black and pink jewel."

Le charme inattendu d'un bijou rose et noir.[1]

Le Buveur d'absinthe was refused at the Salon of 1859 and
Baudelaire was unable to give the public his opinion of it.

[1] The unexpected charm of a pink and black jewel.
"Lola de Valence."

Furthermore, since he was never again asked to write his opinions of the Salons, he was never able to use these discussions as a defense for Manet as he had done for Delacroix. At the Salon of 1861, Manet's portraits of Monsieur and Madame Manet were admitted and *L'Espagnole jouant de la guitare* received honorable mention. The real uproar came, of course, in 1863, on the occasion of the refusal of *Le Déjeuner sur l'herbe* and the subsequent attack on the morality of the picture, a paraphrase of Giorgione's *Concert* at the Louvre, of which no one said anything. Baudelaire was disgusted and pointed out to Manet that this was but one more example of the militant imbecility of the French. Manet painted and engraved portraits of Baudelaire with the droop of the mouth which had now become characteristic.

At this time, also, Baudelaire became very closely associated with Constantin Guys. Guys had come to Paris after successfully making drawings of the Crimean campaign for the *London Illustrated News*; and his drawings of Parisian life had attracted a great deal of attention in the throng of illustrated papers which were giving at the time so much space to the work of Monnier, Daumier and other caricaturists and commentators on the French scene. Baudelaire, impressed with the genius of Guys, made it a point to get in touch with him. The two men became great friends and spent a good deal of time talking and walking along the quays. Baudelaire particularly admired "the modernity" of Guys, that is to say, his ability to seize the most salient characteristics of Parisian actuality. He offered to write an extended study of Guys; but Guys, somewhat alarmed at being made a subject of public comment, agreed to the study provided that, in it, Baudelaire referred to him simply as "Monsieur G."

Le Figaro, Baudelaire's greatest enemy in the press, agreed to take the article. Bourdin, who had violently attacked

Baudelaire more than once, announced that "*Le Figaro* is richer for a study by Monsieur Baudelaire. We have often handled Monsieur Baudelaire roughly, but we keep our doors open to talent. This critique is unusual and distinctly original."

The article gave Baudelaire an opportunity not only to point out the subtleties of the genius of Guys, but also to generalize some of his own attitudes, which, for the most part, were those of his youth. He observes that Guys, moving through theatres, salons, wandering through boulevards and alleys of the Bois, had not only caught the spirit of the nineteenth century: the dominance of the soldier in tunic and képi, the triumphant vulgarity of the bourgeois in his brilliant equipages, the decadence of the silk-hatted dandy and the powerful but purely decorative place of crinolined women in the new society: but had expressed these circumstances with "a suggestion of the eternal." It was his ability to do this that made Guys the artist rather than the mere historian; for, true art contains both the "inconstancy of the flesh and the immortality of the soul."

Guys, an experienced recorder of military life, had certainly caught the pompousness and cockiness of the soldiers of the Second Empire, so emphatic a part of their times in their red and blue and with their great moustaches. They seemed, by their strut and bearing, to know how much the shaky Empire and the new wealth of the new order depended upon them. Guys, too, had clearly recorded the contradictions, the ironies, the aspirations of the new dominating class, which, in attempting to enforce respect for religion, to dictate taste and morality, laid itself open to attack for all sorts of incongruities and hypocrisies.

But it was in his portrayal of the dandy and women that Baudelaire thought Guys had made his most forceful contribution. Guys had caught in the "sad, proud" figure of the dandy, who stood between a dying aristocracy and a rising tide of democracy, "the last gleam of heroism in decay," "the superb but cold sunset" of "these last representatives of human pride." Guys had suggested the wealth and leisure of this rapidly disappearing figure; the "distinction and simplicity of his clothes," which were the symbol of the superiority of his mind; the concealed but obvious distinction of manner when he drove through the Bois; his satisfaction at astonishing the badaud and never being surprised himself, and his cold enmity for the ugly, the stupid and the trivial. He had suggested, too, in picturing the dandy's contact with women, an angry regret at the passing of the feeling that love was "a charming caprice," and the prevalence of the new assumption that it must be either "a truckman's orgy" or "a conjugal duty." Baudelaire hoped that, from the remnants of these men, "a new species of aristocracy" might yet be founded who could survive in the midst of the levelling and spiritual destruction of the new progress.

In his treatment of women, Baudelaire felt that Guys had shown how the nineteenth century woman had revolted against the eighteenth century philosophy of naturalness. He had pictured her "a trifle stupid, perhaps, but dazzling in the general harmony of movement, color, clouds of light and material, with metal and mineral adding to the natural beauty of her eyes." "The dominance of woman over all the conceptions of man," her divinity, her attraction are inseparable from maquillage, costume and artificial attitude. Baudelaire argued that perhaps the nineteenth century woman had done more than any single force to prove the frivolity of the theory of the beneficence of nature and to help in the recovery from the moral and intellectual blindness brought on by the eighteenth century's "denial of original sin"; for she has always known that style, which is a modification and a concealment of nature, is an "aspiration to the ideal." She has always borrowed from the arts and used artificiality "to rise above the natural." So, too, man must admit again that vice and crime are natural; that virtue and religion are requisite artificialities and that, after all, "we have always had the Gods as our teachers." In his literature at any rate there was not the hesitation about the religious conviction, which, in his life, he was achieving slowly, then rejecting, because he could not yet subordinate to it his terrific ambition.

xxxii

THE APPEARANCE of this study, which, because of its length, was published in three installments in *Le Figaro,* did not arouse any comment in the press whatever.

Baudelaire began to think that he was being forgotten. In addition to the article on Guys, he had published a review in *Le Boulevard* of Hugo's *Les Misérables.* Disgusted with the "false morality" of the book, he had written to his mother that "proficient in the art of lying," he had constrained himself as a matter of policy to give a favorable impression of it. He had written that "Hugo is goodness joined to strength," that "his deep voice of charity" is heard "above the permanent accompaniment of the orchestra of all his works"; that, ordinarily, morality in Hugo's books is subordinated, but here "it stands forth" in its own right; and "books of this nature are never useless." But Baudelaire could not help adding, "alas for original sin; even after so many centuries of progress, there seem always sufficient traces of it to remind us of its immemorial reality."

Le Boulevard had also published a new group of poems. In "L'Imprévu," the clock warns the flesh of its decay:

> . . . J'avertis en vain la chair infecte.
> L'homme est aveugle, sourd, fragile comme un mur
> Qu'habite et que ronge un insecte.[1]

---

[1] . . . I warn in vain the rotten flesh,
Man is blind, deaf, fragile as a wall
In which an insect lives and gnaws.
        "L'Imprévu."

Satan, "enormous and ugly as the world," is a reminder that one cannot play a double game both with him and God, and that he will come to claim his own. But an angel "sounds the victory of those whose heart has said, "Blessed be Thy lash, Lord! Blessed be pain, Father! My soul is not a vain thing in Thy hands and Thy prudence is infinite':

> . . . Que béni soit ton fouet,
> Seigneur! Que la douleur, O Père soit bénie!
> Mon âme dans tes mains n'est pas un vain jouet,
> Et ta prudence est infinie.' " [1]

"L'Examen de minuit" is a consideration of his present spiritual condition taken alone at midnight. He admitted that he "had insulted what he loved and flattered what he hated," had "bowed to enormous stupidity"; adored "dull matter"; "drunk without thirst and eaten without hunger"; lived "like a heretic," and "had blasphemed Jesus, the most incontestable of all the Gods."

> . . . blasphémé Jésus
> Des Dieux le plus incontestable!

The sense of God and of his own humanity had never been better expressed in his poems; but he was still concerned with what the world would think of them.

The attitude of editors like De Calonne and Buloz, who had refused the poems in prose because there "was no public for them," had begun to disturb Baudelaire. He began to be in terror of being "forgotten in his own time." He was happy that two thousand copies of Flaubert's latest book, *Salâmbo*,

---

[1] . . . Blessed be Thy lash,
   Lord, may pain, O Father, be blessed!
   My soul in Thy hands is not a vain thing,
   And Thy prudence is infinite.
                    "L'Imprévu."

had succeeded in being sold in two days; for while "it had a good deal of bric-a-brac, it had majesty"; and it certainly deserved success more than the works of those "intellectual sluts," De Musset and Béranger. The Chevalier de Châtelain had written at the instance of his "young secretary, Stéphane Mallarmé," to ask Baudelaire's advice about a translation of Poe's "Raven," which he was doing. A young Roumanian poet sent a vehement letter of admiration. But these did not satisfy him for the sort of recognition he wished. *L'Opinion nationale* had taken a short article by him on the death of Delacroix but had not yet paid him though nearly a year had passed. He conferred to no purpose with Nestor Roqueplan, director of the Imperial Ballet, about the possibility of creating a ballet out of his "Don Juan aux enfers."

Meantime his personal affairs had grown distinctly worse. In spite of the fact that Baudelaire flaunted before Ancelle the possibility of his being involved in a grosse affaire which would take him "out of trusteeship in six weeks," every penny he had earned by his writing had gone into the apparently bottomless maw of his creditors. Jeanne had been making constant demands, even going so far as to say when he sent her money for her expenses at a maison de santé, that she had not received it, so as to make him pay double. *La Revue européenne, La Revue fantaisiste* and *La Revue de Genève,* which had accepted work from him, went out of publication; and he found himself with manuscripts on his hands for which he had not been paid and for which there was no other market. On top of this, Poulet-Malassis had gone bankrupt, was confined in the hospital of the debtors' prison at Madelonnettes with an attack of a serious disease, and had been forced to give Baudelaire's notes to his creditors. Baudelaire now owed Poulet-Malassis five thousand francs. Poulet-Malassis had wished to settle this debt by taking over in perpetuity the copyright of *Les Fleurs du mal*. Baudelaire would not agree, feeling that the book was worth immeasurably more. Meantime, Pincebourde, the clerk in the Paris book-shop of Poulet-Malassis, who in Baudelaire's eyes was something of a Uriah Heep, had bought out Poulet-Malassis and was threatening Baudelaire with legal action in connection with the debt and with the copyright of *Les Fleurs du mal*.

Toward the end of 1863, Baudelaire took stock of himself. He had not won the glory he had expected to win with *Les Fleurs du mal*. He felt that France had not given him due recognition "as it had not to Flaubert and Balzac." Then he had not won the fortune he had counted upon as a concommitant of his glory. On the contrary, he was more in debt than at any other time, not only to Pincebourde, the usual creditors, shopkeepers and hotel owners, but to his mother as well. He estimated that he owed her alone some fifteen thousand francs, begged from her in little sums over a period of fifteen years. It was not that she was asking the return of the money; but he felt humiliated that he could not repay her, particularly since he had always promised her, "that this is the last time that I shall have to ask you. I feel that the month which is opening will bring a decided change in my finances." He spent hours figuring "on little bits of paper." He estimated that if he could earn six thousand francs a year, he would be able to amortize his debts, and, in time, succeed in living a little better than a "hunted werewolf."

He was now forty-two years old. His hair was gray and he resented bitterly, on one of their rare encounters, Sainte-Beuve's calling him "my dear child." His health had grown steadily worse. He worried about the condition of his mind. There were nights of terrible fevers, terrific pains in the head which compelled him to work with his head bound in towels soaked with sedative solutions. There were the terrible cramps, the vomiting "for no apparent reason." He did not know what a night's rest was. During the day he would fall across his bed into a kind of sleep which was not a sleep but a lethargy in which he heard the sounds in the street, the footsteps in the corridor. He would rise in the morning more exhausted than when he went to bed. There were still those falls in which he would bring down with him furniture and curtains. Once he fell in the street, was carried to the doctor's where he had another attack. The doctor prescribed valerian, cold baths and "peace of mind."

Then there was that frightful moment when his mind was brushed "by the wings of imbecility." He remained in a kind of stupor for days, no longer conscious of the passing of time. He came suddenly to himself again "after days."

Baudelaire began to brood about the death of his half-brother, Claude-Alphonse, whom he hated because he had injured him somehow, not out of malice but "out of stupidity." He had died at Fontainebleau of a diabetic condition. Baudelaire, at first, angry that death had released his brother "while some one more deserving still suffered," went to the funeral. Claude-Alphone Baudelaire, at the time of the division of François Baudelaire's fortune, had chosen to take his share in Paris real estate, while Baudelaire had insisted upon his share being in ready cash. With the crowding of the city, which new industrial development under the Empire had brought, the properties increased their value five-fold. Claude-Alphonse, a respected magistrate in the quiet town of Fontainebleau, had made himself a comfortable home with the income from this property. It was meeting for the first time his brother's wife at the funeral which most affected him. It was incomprehensible to him that a man like his brother could have found such a gentle, charming person. Baudelaire insisted that his mother should take Claude-Alphonse's wife to live with her at Honfleur;

for all her pleas, he told his mother that he would not return there until he had wiped out his debt.

It was upon meeting his mother here that he was reminded of the great disparity between her age and his father's. Upon their marriage there had been thirty-three years difference between them. To this disproportion, Baudelaire insisted upon attributing the present feebleness of his body and the uncertain condition of his mind. "I am the child of an old man" he cried to his mother. He wrote to Georges Barral, "You are a student of physiology with Claude Bernard. Ask him what he thinks of the fruit of such a marriage." To inheritance from his father, he attributed the death of Claude-Alphonse, who, in addition to a diabetic condition, had suffered a mental relapse. Baudelaire recalled his childhood in his first home in the ancient Hôtel d'Alègre on the Rue Hautefeuille, where, in the large faded rooms, he believed he remembered seeing the ghosts of "idiot and maniacal ancestors."

He returned to Paris in a state of extreme nervous intensity. He was in the midst of completing the translation of Poe's *Eureka*. The proofs would be frequently piled on his table for days. Then he would attack them, sometimes working all night. He translated this work of Poe with his usual attention to detail and to exactitude of language; but perhaps with the least enthusiasm. This philosophic effort did not wholly convince him. He felt that the book would require a foreword from some well-known literary personality to make it at all attractive to the public. Taine, at that time, because of his *Histoire de la littérature anglaise,* was considered an authority on English and American letters. It was for this reason that Baudelaire appealed to him for a foreword. Taine declined with thanks, declaring that he was exceptionally busy at the moment. The book appeared without attracting any great critical attention. *La Petite Revue* observed that, while Baudelaire's translation seemed to be excellent, the substance of the book was dull and incomprehensible. Baudelaire was touched by a valiant effort in *Le Moniteur* at a metaphysical analysis of *Eureka,* which was written by Théophile Gautier's daughter, Judith, whom he had known since she was a little girl.

In March, 1864, three poems, "Bien loin d'ici," "Les Yeux de Berthe" and "Sur le Tasse en prison," appeared in *La Revue nouvelle.* "Sur le Tasse en prison" had been accepted in 1844 by *Le Bulletin des Amis des arts,* which did not survive long enough to publish it. The poem was an explanation and a defense of a picture of the same name by Delacroix. It celebrated "that genius locked in prison" as a soul of dark dreams "whom reality stifles":

> Que le Réel étouffe entre ses quatre murs [1]

'Bien loin d'ici" seems, too, to have been of an earlier date because it speaks of Dorothée, a memory of his voyage to L'Ile-de-Bourbon, at ease among her flowers and cushions:

> Et son coude dans les coussins
> Écoute pleurer les bassins. . . .[2]

"Les Yeux de Berthe," also, was an old manuscript originally entitled "Les Yeux de mon enfant" and dedicated later "to that horrible little girl" he was to meet in Brussels. Baudelaire was writing nothing new at this time. He offered to give a series of lectures at Le Théâtre des Italiens on his contemporaries. His offer was refused. Some poems in prose, which *Le Figaro* had taken, were returned by the editor who said that "they were beginning to bore the public."

[1] Whom reality stifles within its four walls
    "Sur le Tasse en prison."
[2] And with her elbow in the cushions
    Listens to the weeping of the fountains. . . .
        "Bien loin d'ici."

xxxiii

IT WAS THIS LAST TOUCH which made him decide to leave France. He despised "the face of a Frenchman." He would go to Belgium and see what he could save from the ruin. Théophile Gautier remarked, "Why go to Belgium? When I travel, I travel for pleasure." But Belgium was the place to which everybody went who was in exile from France. Hugo was there. Poulet-Malassis was in Brussels, this time really publishing obscene books, or, at any rate, the more piquant eighteenth century masters like Andréa de Nerciat and Choderlos de Laclos, and also political attacks on the Second Empire like *Les Propos de Labénius.* He would get all his works together and sell them to a Belgian publisher. Meantime, so as not to lose every oportunity, he would see what he could do to place his complete works in Paris through a literary agent. After a great deal of thought, he selected Julien Lemer to take care of his literary interests in Paris. He would be his own literary agent in Brussels. He had already written to the publishing house of Lacroix and Verboeckoven at Brussels, laying his proposal before them. It was the firm which had just brought out Hugo's *Les Misérables*; and Baudelaire further wrote to Hugo, asking him to put in a word for him with the company.

Baudelaire explained to Lemer and Lacroix and Verboeckoven that he had five volumes to offer. The translations of Poe were out of the transaction because financial pressure had compelled him to give up all rights to these to Michel Lévy for two thousand francs ready cash. This step Baudelaire regretted bitterly because these books sold well and he saw "an annual loss of five hundred francs." He had no intention of giving his books away so cheaply again. He was after his "six thousand francs a year." Hetzel had taken an option for a third edition of *Les Fleurs du mal,* provided Baudelaire could supply him with a second volume of verse within five years. But, as this was tentative, he listed his books as follows: *Les Fleurs du mal,* which he felt was the best of all his work, would live the longest and must therefore be sold at the best price; *Les Paradis artificiels*; the unfinished poems in prose to which he had given the title of *Spleen de Paris*; a volume of his literary criticism, called provisionally, "Réflexions sur mes contemporaines"; "L'Art romantique," a collection of his "Salons" and all his art criticism. He wanted, if possible, to sell these to one publisher; and, with the income from them added to what he would earn from publication of projected plays, books and occasional poems and articles, to enjoy some relief from financial pressure.

In his determination to solve his money problems as quickly as possible, he contemplated two other sources of income. One, which made him "shudder to think of it," was "to give lessons." The other, much more attractive, was to give a series of lectures on art and literature. His friend, the artist Alfred Stevens, who lived on and off in Belgium, had impressed Baudelaire with a possibility of making a living in this way. He had particularly emphasized the considerable sums which Dickens and Thackeray had earned in their tours of the United States. Because Baudelaire had already prepared the beginnings of such a series of lectures based upon his critical writing, in the hope of capturing a contract at Le Théâtre des Italiens, Alfred Stevens, through Poulet-Malassis in Belgium, immediately got in touch with Monsieur Vervoort who was not only President of Le Cercle artistique of Belgium, but President of the Belgian Chamber of Deputies as well.

The response was extremely gratifying. Monsieur Vervoort would be delighted to have Baudelaire give a series of lectures on the literary and artistic subjects indicated not only in Brussels but in all the other cities of Belgium which had branches of the Society, for the considerable sum of two hundred francs a lecture. Monsieur Vervoort did not enclose a contract; but Baudelaire felt that he could have faith in a man of Vervoort's position. And at, perhaps, "the darkest and most solemn year-end" of his life, he wrote his mother that he still had hope of "fortune, glory and vengeance." He added in the letter that in his stay in Belgium he would complete, among others, a projected book, *Mon coeur mis à nu,* a title suggested in Poe's "Marginalia," in which, "while respecting my mother and even my step-father," he would tell of his training, how his ideas were fashioned; would make it incessantly felt how much he was "a stranger to the world and its pursuits"; would turn against France his "real talent for impertinence," and would deliver himself of all his bitterness. This would make him, "perhaps, feel better."

In spite of all his efforts to be independent before he left, his mother had to help him get out of his hotel and to silence some of his louder creditors. The two thousand francs which Michel Lévy had given him for perpetual rights to his translations of Poe had long before gone into the hands of creditors. He was being sued by De Calonne for some complex financial transaction connected with an advance payment on some poems. Jeanne was nagging from her maison de santé and still attempting to cheat him. He gave all the available money to make her comfortable and promised more as soon as he earned more in Belgium. "Belgium," he told his mother, "will pay for everything." He also told her that the prospects of the trip terrified him a little. He "did not have absolute confidence in the Belgians"; but he must leave. He would not return until he could repay her. He would take no more from her even if he died. He did not wish to see France again until it asked for him.

Taking only "necessary books," leaving the rest at Honfleur with his pictures and bibelots, with a somewhat worn wardrobe and a railroad pass which he had somehow come by, he left Paris for Brussels on April 23, 1864.

xxxiv

IN SPITE OF THE terrible illness which so much immobilized him with pain, which cut so deeply into his time, which "would not permit him to write more than fifty lines of prose" without having his mind confused, he set out his books and papers resolutely on the table in his new room at the Hôtel du Grand Miroir at 28 Rue de la Montagne, in Brussels with the feeling that a new life of sorts was beginning and that anything but success was unthinkable. He had taken a modest seven franc room, going for his meals to the cheaper restaurants like Bienvenu's where the fifteen-sous meal, detestable at its best to him, was almost inedible. Feeling that wine was perhaps too much of a stimulant for the condition of his health, he drank only faro, a kind of beer, the "abominable taste" of which frequently made him ill.

Upon his arrival, he immediately wrote letters to the publishers, Lacroix and Verboeckoven, arranging for an interview; to Le Cercle artistique, making final preparations for the first of the series of lectures, which was to be on the first of May and on the subject of Delacroix; to Lemer, urging him to use every available pressure to dispose of his works in France, suggesting Les Frères Garnier as the first likely market.

He set out to put order in his life. He worked as assiduously as his health permitted. He avoided taking credit in the shops and restaurants. He eliminated from his diet all stimulants, taking laudanum only for the terrific neuralgic pains. When he was not writing, he spent hours in the cabinet de lecture of Monsieur Bluff at 10 Rue du Midi. For social contacts, he immediately looked up Poulet-Malassis, who lived some distance away on la Rue de Mercellis in the Faubourg d'Ixelles.

He looked up the Hugos, who had opened a spacious house on la Rue de l'Astronomie in le Quartier Saint-Josse where they held every Wednesday a huge gathering of admirers. Victor Hugo welcomed him in his usual loud way, but was able to give him no more than the few minutes he gave to each one on the long line of artists and poets who came to drink his tea and shake his hand. Madame Hugo was much more warm and personal in her reception. In a letter to his mother, Baudelaire called them both stupid, a qualification he was to soften later in the case of Madame Hugo, when she took so much interest in his care during his illness. Baudelaire could not bear the echoes of the father's philosophy of Progress and International Education which he heard in the sons, Charles and François-Victor, and even in Charles's wife. He wrote his mother that if he had children that aped him like that, he would strangle them. In line with Hugo's alleged love for music, he had installed a piano in the salon, at which Charles's wife would play, what were to Baudelaire, some of the trivialities of Meyerbeer and Offenbach, or some of the "loud pieces" of which Hugo was fond. But when the principal musicale was ended, Baudelaire would ask Madame Charles Hugo to play over and over some of his favorite passages from Wagner.

He had also met Berthe, the young woman to whom he rededicated his poem, "Les Yeux de mon enfant," and in whose great eyes he thought he saw at first so much purity and candor,

> Je ne sais quoi de bon, de doux. . . .[1]

[1] I know not what of good and sweet. . . .
   "Les Yeux de Berthe."

Their association was quickly terminated: serving Baudelaire supper, and finding him preoccupied with the movement of some clouds, she cried, "Eat your supper, you damned cloud-gaper!" That was the end. He became a familiar figure at Horton's, at la Brasserie du Prince de Galles. Dining at Bienvenu's, he would meet Alfred Stevens, Bancel and other Frenchmen in enforced or voluntary exile from the Empire, for some "human conversation"; for he already had begun to suspect "the stupidity of the Belgians."

XXXV

BELGIUM HAD ALREADY BEGUN to appear to him another France, only worse. Belgium was about to celebrate the anniversary of the Revolution of 1830. It was about to celebrate the success of the philosophy of Progress. The Belgian press reeked even more than the French with stories of crime. The Belgian bourgeois was not only stupid but unbearably pompous. Hugo was the favorite poet of the Belgians. Anticlericalism was rampant. God did not compare with the steam-engine. Even the Belgian universities seemed to be attempting to reduce God to nothing, to "eliminate the Judge," and, in this way, "to imagine that they had abolished sin." He was irritated to read in one of the papers this line of reasoning by a certain free-thinking professor by the name of Flouren: "In the imagination of poets, humanity usually begins with a golden age, a state of happiness from which it is not long in falling. In religious fictions, this same false idea is found. Science shows us, on the contrary, peoples living a life, at first bestial, and then slowly, often with interruption, but always with constant certainty, achieving the inevitable upward Progress of our species."

The great modern painter of Belgium was a person by the name of Wiertz, who was not only a disciple of Progress, but a painter given acutely to le poncif, and much worse than poor old Vernet and others whom he had so roughly handled in his "Salons." Félicien Rops, whom he met sometime later, was the only painter whom he considered of any artistic integrity. The writers of Belgium appeared to him a motley and nondescript lot, mostly given, in the name of realism, to deliberate obscenity. There was alas, even a Belgian imitator of Béranger by the name of Bovie.

He began to be more and more irritated by the grinning obsequiousness of shopkeepers, the oily pompousness which overlaid the bourgeois victory in Belgium. As for the Belgian masses, "Imbecility was marked upon their faces." In them, he found a perfect mingling of "stubbornness and stupidity." They were loud and dirty; they "laughed at the sad and grew sad at the joyful"; and, with their "thin legs, great red hands and enormous necks, the Belgian women made him ill to look at them.

Baudelaire got himself into difficulties with the Belgian public almost at once. Soon after he arrived, there was a celebration of the three hundredth anniversary of the birth of Shakespeare. Baudelaire took umbrage at some of the reports he read of the goings-on at a banquet for this occasion at which Hugo was the guest of honor. He wrote a letter to the press, saying that, among other things, the guests at this occasion would have done well to get the facts and names of Shakespeare's plays straight, and, at least, to spell his name correctly. There was something of an uproar in which Baudelaire was accused of insulting Hugo.

Then a squad of police, led by an over-pompous brigadier, descended upon Baudelaire's lodgings at the Hôtel du Grand Miroir and began to cross-examine him as to what purpose (other than "to write," as indicated in the fiche filed with the local police) had really brought him to Belgium. Baudelaire, irritated that the brigadier would not believe that this was his sole purpose, angrily shouted at them that he had murdered his father and that the French Police had made a deal with him, agreeing, if he would act as a spy for them on French exiles in Brussels, to let him come to

Belgium unmolested. Baudelaire was amazed that now the brigadier believed him. Indeed, the news got about; and, whenever Baudelaire appeared in cafés and restaurants, French exiles watched him with considerable uneasiness.

xxxvi

THE FIRST NEWS HE RECEIVED was from Le Cercle artistique. His initial lecture, announced for the first of May, had been postponed. This news unnerved him considerably because he had keyed himself up for this occasion. This was to be his first experience on the lecture platform. He had rewritten with care his paper on Delacroix, trying to make it meet the exigencies of time, and had worried whether he would get his effects as well by the spoken as by the written word. The matter of clothes had troubled him also. He had been informed that some sort of dress attire would be de rigueur. This was out of the question for him: the best he could do would be to brush up and have mended his old clothes, which were black anyway, and put on a white tie for the occasion. He wished to make a good impression. If he could make a success of his first series of lectures, he foresaw the possibility of becoming a regular lecturer in Belgium, doing the tour annually from Brussels, through Antwerp, Bruges, Liège to Gand, in this way assuring himself an income of at least two thousand francs a year. Upon his arrival in Brussels, Baudelaire had even written to the branches in these cities, "notifying them of my presence." He had not heard from any of them. He was also worried lest his health might not be sufficiently good on the advanced date. He wrote to his mother at this time that he had been "constantly ill for weeks," sometimes being unable to go out for days. By a terrible effort of will and nerves, he had made himself feel equal to the lecture at the arranged time and now it was postponed.

He was waiting, too, with impatience, for some answer to his letter to the firm of Lacroix and Verboeckoven, requesting an interview concerning the possible sale of his complete works to them. The three weeks which had passed without an answer to his letter made him feel that perhaps "enemies in Paris had reached Lacroix and Verboeckoven." He had even written personal letters to the two members of the firm, inviting them to his lecture. There had been no answer to these, as yet, either.

The news from Lemer in Paris was promising but always vague. Lemer had been to the offices of Garnier Frères, but had not been able to have an interview with either of the brothers. Baudelaire was becoming nervous at the slowness of the proceedings. He wrote to Monsieur Lejoysne, a friend of the Meurices, with valuable relations in the financial and literary world, requesting him to use his influence to stimulate the Garniers.

He now took a different tone in his correspondence with Ancelle. Time and distance were responsible for the change. Writing to Ancelle that he expected the lectures and the success of "a big deal," to make him soon independent financially, he also communicated with him on more equal and amicable terms, discussing current books, the international crisis, in which Italy and Cavour were playing such an important rôle, and exchanging views on religion with him. Baudelaire would now even inquire with honest concern about the health of Madame Ancelle and of the little pimply boy who was now quite a young man. He wrote to Ancelle that he was the only person he had insulted for twenty years and upon whose friendship he could still count.

In these first weeks of waiting in Brussels, Baudelaire again became bound closely to Poulet-Malassis. While

"Coco" lived some distance away from Baudelaire, they came together rather frequently to dine and talk. There had been something of a breach at the time of the bankruptcy. Poulet-Malassis, under the influence of his brother-in-law, had begun to feel that perhaps after all, what with the extensive advances which he had made to Baudelaire and which had not been repaid or liquidated by the sale of *Les Fleurs du mal* or *Les Paradis artificiels,* Baudelaire was in part responsible for the collapse. Baudelaire had been angry with Poulet-Malassis for putting such a small ultimate value as five thousand francs upon *Les Fleurs du mal.*

But here in exile the breach was healed. Baudelaire would have liked to dine as often as possible with Poulet-Malassis, if Poulet-Malassis had not lived so far away, not only because his eating-place was immensely superior to any he had found, but also because he preferred the conversation of Frenchmen. Poulet-Malassis, on his part, reminded Baudelaire that they were veterans of the barricades of 1848. While Baudelaire was in no sentimentally reminiscent mood about this adventure, he felt that he owed a great deal to Poulet-Malassis; that, as bad as things were, "he would not have been known without him."

The two therefore resumed their camaradarie which was stimulated by a distinct but amicable difference of opinion upon spiritual matters. Poulet-Malassis clung still to Voltaireism and was still an ardent and obscenely witty anti-clerical. Baudelaire admitted that the sight of some of the gross Belgian clerics was enough to turn anybody against the Church; but, at the same time, Belgium was becoming so crassly anti-Christian, so vulgarly and enthusiastically materialistic that he was "driven, out of the spirit of contradiction, to defend Jesuitism and to become devout." But, under pressure from Poulet-Malassis, he began to admit that he "really did not know what the Divine Will was," what, if anything, God intended; that the Divine Will was separated from his spirit by "doubt and anguish"; but that, "since no one knows exactly whether his acts respond to the Will of God, one should, nevertheless, observe the strictest rules of morality." He still feared to embrace the divine truth which he knew and met it with intellectualization in the conversation of a moment.

Meantime, the day scheduled for his first lecture arrived. This time there was no postponement. Baudelaire worked over the paper all day. His health had not been of the best, the pains and dizziness continuing in spite of all the specifics the pharmacist sold him. He spent the day making himself presentable. His clothes were in the best condition that mending and pressing could bring them to. In a high state of nervousness, precisely at quarter to eight he left his hotel, with his manuscript under his arm, a dazzling white tie, his tall hat and stick and wearing his Inverness cape because of the "freezing Belgian spring." He was in the small room just off the platform even before the person who was to introduce him arrived.

The lecture was to be held in the Gothic palace just opposite the Town Hall of Brussels. The lecture-room was on the second floor. As Baudelaire entered, he observed with some bitterness that only the Belgians would have thought of setting aside the ground floor of this ancient and beautiful building for the selling of hay, grain and feed and for the business of selling song-birds in little cages. His first view of the hall where he was to speak was not prepossessing. It was scarcely lit by a few, smoky oil-lamps suspended from the ceiling, one, fortunately, over a small lectern on the lecturer's platform. The walls were bare of any decoration whatever, and were streaked and black as if they had been frequently exposed to the weather. In front of the platform was a series of rough wooden benches on which he was pleased to see a fairly large crowd of people: but as a crowd they were silent and unwelcoming.

When he began to speak, his rather high-pitched voice came back to him so sharply from the vaulted ceiling that he was somewhat disconcerted. He pulled himself together, however, and continued his clear exposition and defense of the genius of Delacroix. When he had finished, a number of people came to the platform to shake his hand. He was somewhat upset that none of them turned out to be Lacroix or Verboeckoven. He was considerably disturbed, too, by the attitude of the curious. "They expected to see a monster and ended by believing I had not written my own book." Baudelaire recalled that he should have been prepared for this sort of reception from Belgian intellectuals; for he had gone, in order to get some idea of how to go about a lecture, to a talk by Alexander Dumas, père, and had been shocked, after the lecture, to see the Belgians giggling behind Dumas' back and making ill-mannered jokes about his color. Baudelaire, while not considering Dumas a true literary artist, felt that he deserved the respect of the world for his magnificent "African energy" and for "the special kind of delight" which nobody could deny was in his books. He returned home from his lecture, upset by unpleasant questions and incredulous stares, and was more than ever angered with the Belgians.

He was somewhat surprised the next morning to read in *L'Indépendance Belge,* a laudatory article about his lecture, written by Monsieur Frédérix in his column entitled "Les Beaux-Arts." He immediately wrote to Frédérix, thanking him for his considerate article.

Because of this, he felt that he had one foot at least planted firmly on the way toward the financial progress he wished to make in Belgium. He wrote to Ancelle that the lecture was a "distinct triumph for him"; but, to his mother, he confided that, though "they say that my first lecture was a great success," he was depressed at the infinity of "empty skulls" and "the slowness" with which everything was moving.

By the time of the second lecture, Baudelaire had made up his mind to sell to Lacroix and Verboeckoven only three of his volumes, *Les Paradis artificiels,* his criticism on art and his criticism on literature for "twenty thousand francs, or as much as possible, for five years." But there was no word from them yet, either in answer to his request for an interview, or to his invitation to the second lecture. He had also decided to write a book about his trip to Belgium and had already written a letter to *Le Figaro,* asking whether they would be interested in publishing sections of it as he completed them.

The second lecture was scheduled for the eleventh of May. Baudelaire had rewritten his estimate of Théophile Gautier to meet the time requirement of a two-hour lecture. He was considerably dismayed to find an audience of about twenty people. The political preoccupations raised by the approach of a general election probably accounted for the small audience. Furthermore, Baudelaire's personality and ideas did not appeal to the rank and file of Le Cercle artistique. He was not a colorful political martyr of the Second Empire like Bancel, Ranc and Madier de Montjau, who had come to talk to them about democracy; he was not a follower of Proudhon like the flamboyant Deschanel. In any case, Baudelaire was disconcerted by the smallness of the audience and by the fact that most of these had gone before he finished. He, however, read on steadily in the cold and almost dark room, as if he did not notice the remnants of the small audience. Those who remained, according to Camille Lemonnier, seemed to suspect every word of Baudelaire, to seek some treacherous thrust behind his excessive praise of Gautier.

Without lifting his eyes from his paper, he declaimed in conclusion, "I salute in Théophile Gautier my master, the great poet of our time." A door slammed in the back of the hall. Baudelaire rapidly made three stiff bows in three directions, and quickly left the lecture room.

At the third lecture on the twenty-first of May, which he was to make on *Les Paradis artificiels,* there were only four people present. According to Charles Tardieu, who had not missed any of the lectures, Baudelaire was in obvious nervous difficulties right from the beginning. His teeth were chattering. He was shaking all over. He stammered, stopped and reread. At the end of the lecture, a uniformed lackey approached and placed a hundred franc note into Baudelaire's hand, saying that this was payment for the lectures; that the other two, on Guys and Poe, need not be given, and that, should Le Cercle be in funds the following year, it would indemnify him for the other four hundred francs.

Behind the lackey, stood a well-dressed, distinguished gentleman, his face full of respect and commiseration. He was Monsieur Prosper Crabbe, a wealthy stock broker of Brussels, who had attended the three lectures and had listened most attentively. When the lackey had gone, he asked Baudelaire if he felt he would care to give another lecture, for a consideration, of course, at his home to which he would invite a number of distinguished and appreciative friends and to which Baudelaire would be at liberty to invite as many others as he chose. Baudelaire accepted Monsieur Crabbe's offer with as much gratitude as he was able to muster at the moment.

xxxvii

BAUDELAIRE WROTE to his mother the next day: "My wonderful trip! For playing a magnanimous rôle with Belgian lawyers, statesmen and artists, I have been robbed. I have no recourse because I did not insist upon a contract. I wanted to give the hundred francs to the poor. It paid my hotel bill, less three sous. But I am going to organize my own series of lectures. A stock broker has done me the favor of permitting me to use his salon. I will only have the best society there. I want public reparation for this stupid ill-treatment. I am told that the head of the King's household will be there . . . You do not know what it costs me to write you this."

Meantime, there had been no news from Lacroix and Verboeckoven. They had not been at the third lecture. Baudelaire invited them to come to hear him at Monsieur Crabbe's.

Baudelaire had already begun his book on Belgium. "Going to bed at nine and rising at five," with as much energy as his illness and his other preoccupations left him, he had begun sketching "the main lines" which the book was to take, and to read the "hundreds of volumes" necessary to the undertaking. He planned to make a political, historical, artistic and religious survey of this kingdom of "brutes." He would visit every important city and then show Belgium to the world. He wrote to *Le Figaro,* making his intentions more precise concerning his projected articles on Belgium. *Le Figaro* answered that they would not be interested in material which attacked a "sister democracy." But this refusal did not deter him. He wrote to other French papers, offering the articles. He informed Lemer, who still had nothing definite from the Garniers, that he could offer along with the other volumes, this projected new book to which he was giving tentatively the title of "Pauvre Belgique!"

In the notes he was already setting down with bitterness and vehemence, he observed that in all classes of Belgian society, dishonesty was a "form of honor"; that not only were the bodies of Belgians dirty but their souls as well, and that it was not for nothing that the most common crime in Belgium was rape; that Belgium was unworthy of all the Christian art and philosophy showered upon it.

It was time for his lecture at Prosper Crabbe's. Upon entering Monsieur Crabbe's enormous salon, Baudelaire was overwhelmed with the "almost laughable" profusion of flowers and little cakes. He observed that there were about "ten or twelve depressed people" lounging on the sofas, waiting for him to begin his lecture on poetry and to hear him read from his own work. When he began, he saw that he did not have their attention. Upon his saying something about Christianity, he caught one of the brokers observing to another, "You see! He calls us crétins." Baudelaire continued talking and reading for some ten minutes during which his audience became even more inattentive. In the middle of a sentence, laughing a little, he threw up his hands, and said, "Let's leave it at that"; and went hastily toward the cakes and sandwiches.

Monsieur Crabbe did not give up interest in Baudelaire, however. Sensing Baudelaire's financial troubles, he invited him to put in order his fine library of old and expensive editions. Baudelaire completed the work, but afterwards declined any further aid from Monsieur Crabbe.

xxxviii

HE **WROTE TO HIS MOTHER** the news of this debacle and told her "that he had made up his mind that he simply would not leave his hotel room"; that he "would see no one." Still, this was impossible; for in between his working on his autobiography, *Mon coeur mis à nu,* on a proposed translation of the *Satyricon* for Poulet-Malassis, he was giving a great deal of time to making notes and gathering material for his book on Belgium which required his visiting all the principal Belgian cities.

The first city he had visited was Antwerp. He had been delighted with the beauty of the place, "but the people here are as imbecile as in Brussels." He next proposed a trip to see the town and battlefield of Waterloo. Nadar, who, to his capacity as journalist and photographer, had added the talent for making balloon ascensions, and who had been invited to go up in his balloon by the Belgian Government in order to celebrate the Revolution of 1830, agreed to accompany Baudelaire. George Barral, an acquaintance of Baudelaire's from Paris, who was passing through Belgium, agreed to go along also.

The three reached Waterloo in September 1864, toward evening and went straight to the Hôtel des Colonnes where Victor Hugo had completed a part of *La Légende des siècles.* The maiden sisters Dehaze, who were the proprietors of the hotel, and to whom the name Baudelaire did not seem to mean anything, showed with great pride and solemnity the room which Hugo had occupied, when "he was writing his great epic." Baudelaire insisted upon having a room over-looking the field of Waterloo which still had vestiges of the disastrous sunken road. Overcome for the moment with Hugo's resonant lines, he intoned for Nadar and Barral the whole poem beginning: "Waterloo, Waterloo, Waterloo, morne plaine." That evening he insisted upon having a gay and somewhat recherché dinner with his companions. Before it was over, however, he took a chill and left at once for Hal where he took the train for Brussels.

xxxix

His illness had taken so sharp a turn for the worse, that he felt it necessary to put himself in the hands of a doctor again. The doctor, a young man by the name of Marx, after listening to Baudelaire's recital of his symptoms, declared that he was suffering from hysteria. "Hysteria!" exclaimed Baudelaire in a letter to his mother, "that is to say, he doesn't know what's the matter."

Baudelaire, nevertheless, followed the doctor's prescriptions, using sedatives and bromides which did not deaden the pain completely, nor did they stop the sudden losing of his balance or check the frightful lapses of his mind. There were moments when he could not read what he had written; or, if he could, would find that he had said often the opposite of his intention. It would take him "an hour to decipher the first few words" of his mother's letter. The night retchings were now a common occurrence which nothing seemed to stop. Yet he would nail himself to his table for hours trying to formulate things which his mind sometimes simply could not retain.

In his lucid moments, he gathered together as much of his strength as he could to finish all the work he had under consideration. There was the last volume of Poe, *Histoires grotesques et sérieuses,* which had already been paid for, little as it was, by Michel Lévy. It was a matter of honor to complete it shortly. But it had to be gone over in the usual meticulous ways. There were the plays, not completed yet, but still a possible source of quick income. There was *Mon*

Coeur mis à nu, an autobiography, which, "because it would make Rousseau's Confessions look pale beside it," ought to bring him considerable income and public attention again; for Baudelaire felt that he was being entirely forgotten. There was "Pauvre Belgique!" which, too, for its frank expression, ought to catch the French public, add to his income, and help to silence his creditors—especially Arondel who kept Baudelaire in constant terror—and give him a few months' peace in France; for he wanted to go home now, but "gloriously" and without debt.

The sale of his other books was, however, not progressing. Only through the good offices of Manet, did Baudelaire get news from Lemer that the business with the Garniers was getting nowhere whatever. He began to fear that failure was certain; that "God and luck" were not on his side; that his name had "no literary value"; that he was the victim of persecution by "the Hugo crowd" and by the publishers in Paris "who must be poisoning the others" against him. He wrote to Ancelle that "failure simply must not be thought of." Ancelle answered in a letter which astonished Baudelaire, professing complete faith in Baudelaire's genius and including a small personal loan.

Every letter he received now inspired him with more terror than before. He even hated to open letters from his mother, so full were these of pleas to "come home and give it all up"; so full were they of reminders of his creditors who were even nagging her. It would anger him to read that she was "praying constantly for him," or to see expressions like "my poor child." In one letter, she wrote that she was so worried that she was coming to Brussels. Terrified of her seeing him in his condition of ill-health and poverty, Baudelaire answered that the troubles he had written to her about were trivial; that her imagination was too active. He was confident that every letter held annoying or bad news.

A letter finally came from Lacroix and Verboeckoven, granting him an interview. In the extremely businesslike offices of the concern, the junior partner, Monsieur Lacroix, flanked by a heavy, florid Fleming, an important stockholder, received him. It seemed to Baudelaire that during the interview they played with him. The superior attitude of the stockholder upset him. The shrewd negativeness of Lacroix angered him. Lacroix declined at once to consider republishing his works; but, "just because he knew I hadn't any," asked him if he had a new novel. Baudelaire asked in a counter-proposal, whether they would consider a translation of the *Melmoth* of Maturin. Lacroix answered that he would take up the matter with Monsieur Verboeckoven.

xl

MEANTIME, BAUDELAIRE CONTINUED his visits to the cities of Belgium. He went next to Malines. He had a pleasant surprise. The town was green and immensely quiet. The church with its fragile chimes, surrounded by the bright houses and backed by deep meadows and fresh skies, overwhelmed him with a sense of peace. He wrote to Ancelle that he would like to die in Malines, "if it were not Belgian."

He returned to Brussels to fall into the deepest sort of depression and spiritual confusion. Under the influence of De Maistre he began to pray—in De Maistre's phrase—"to set out his sentinels for the night."

Manet was being attacked by the press for his *Olympia* and *Le Christ insulté,* and had written Baudelaire, saying that he needed his "healthy judgment" for defense. Baudelaire had answered, urging Manet to bring up all the reserves of his character for the struggle. Then he had written to Madame Meurice, indicating that he feared that Manet's character was too feeble for the fight. As for himself, he told her that he was throwing in every ounce of his strength and his nerves to win and asked the support of her prayers.

Madame Meurice wrote him, attempting to cheer him with news of Manet and of their musical evenings. Her chatter to the effect that he would have enjoyed seeing her in her "Robin Hood gown with its Incroyable jacket," and her efforts at literary snobbishness did not please him, however. Neither did the news from her that Lacroix, taking Baudelaire's suggestion for a translation of Maturin's *Mel-*

moth had given the job to Mademoiselle Judith, an actress at La Comédie Française.

Ancelle, in an effort to divert him, indulged also in bits of literary chit-chat which included news that the younger Dumas had just married. Baudelaire answered, "Serves him right for writing such frightful plays." Ancelle wrote, too, that, he had, in order to keep up with things, gone to hear Deschanel. Baudelaire scolded him for being stupid enough to listen to "a big idiot who does not believe in miracles, only in common sense." And the news that Jeanne was going blind upset him considerably.

xli

HE WAS CERTAIN NOW that he was being forgotten because he was "writing so many letters which remained unanswered." Most of all, he chafed at receiving no news from Lemer; for, with the refusal of Lacroix and Verboeckoven, the only publisher of means and importance in Belgium, it would be absolutely necessary to find a publisher in France. There was nowhere else. He had put the matter in the hands of an agent not only because he would not be in France, but because he felt that a man of this sort could do better financially than he. He had written Lemer several letters of polite inquiry as to the progress of their affair; but he hesitated to write too often for fear of annoying him. But, exasperated after almost a year of half-news and silence, he wrote to Lemer, reminding him politely that, "I exist."

He felt that he had so much to do and so little time. He had "asked God for so many reprieves"; and, yet, he was sure that he had wasted so much time. "Three hundred and sixty-five days in a year and twenty-four hours a day, and yet I have accomplished so little." He had not accomplished glory or wealth. All that was yet to be done. The placing of his complete works with a Paris publisher was his last chance.

Meantime, Hetzel, the publisher who had taken a five-year option on *Les Fleurs du mal,* gave up the option, stating that he felt that he was not able to take the risk at that time. Furthermore, the second book of poetry on which the

153

option depended had not been finished as promised. Baudelaire had already begun preparing a preface to a third edition of *Les Fleurs du mal,* which read: "This book dares to face for the third time the sunlight of public stupidity. Fortunately, I have a character which takes pleasure from hatred and glories in contempt."

He wrote to his mother that his "name did not seem to have any value"; and to Ancelle that no one wanted "that frightful book into which I have put all my heart, my religion, all my hatred"; that his greatest fault was, perhaps, to have had "a talent for depicting evil too well."

Articles which *La Revue de Paris* and *L'Opinion nationale* had accepted were returned because these magazines were running out of funds. *Le Figaro* returned his translation, "Marie Roget," because it was "over the heads of the subscribers." Baudelaire could not place this story anywhere now because *Les Histoires grotesques et sérieuses,* of which it was a part, was shortly to be published in Paris.

He was, indeed, now completing the last painfully meticulous touches to this final translation of the works of Poe. He hoped that its appearance would help to bring his name before the public. He tried with as much haste as his care in correcting would permit, to get the last proof-sheets back to Paris as quickly as possible. The book was published on March 22, 1865. It was received in almost complete silence by the Parisian press. One newspaper deigned to announce in connection with a bald statement of the fact that the book had been published, that Monsieur Baudelaire was preparing a book on Belgium, whose hospitality he was now enjoying, so that he could better "strangle her."

xlii

AT THE BEGINNING of 1865, for all the writing he had already done, and for all his complicated and numerous literary projects—to which he had now added plans for a study of Sainte-Beuve and of Choderlos de Laclos, whose *Liaisons dangereuses* he considered of a perfect and "cruel beauty"— he was not receiving any income whatever. He wrote to his mother that, in spite of this, he was not without courage; that he spent no day without labor; that "the cheerfulness and courage of Poulet-Malassis" helped him; but that the only thing he feared was that he was being forgotten in Paris. He added that now he no longer had any hope of making a fortune from his writing; but that, given four or five years more, his one remaining wish was to pay his debts and make her proud of him. He wanted glory, he continued, not as a vain thing, but, for his old age, "a positive and solid good." He wanted to be back in Paris, to be at Honfleur with her. He missed his room, his books, his pictures; but all talk of a return was "out of the question" until he could tell her definitely that a satisfactory arrangement had been made for the sale of his complete works.

His financial affairs were so bad at this time, however, that he had to think of returning to Paris, not only to stimulate Lemer and to do some soliciting on his own account among the publishers, but to arrange to silence Pincebourde, the Auvergnat clerk who had bought out Poulet-Malassis, who was holding an old note against Baudelaire and was threatening proceedings if he was not satisfied. Baudelaire, who until

155

now, had declined all aid from his mother, insisting that in
Belgium he would manage without recourse to her, was constrained to ask her for nine hundred francs to satisfy Madame
Lepage, the owner of L'Hôtel du Grand Miroir, and to pay
for his trip to Paris. This woman had already begun to torment Baudelaire, spying on his goings and comings and inter-
cepting and opening his mail. He had become ashamed to
ask her to pay any more for his medicine. His mother had
answered, sending the money and saying that perhaps she
should get rid of her maid; for she declared that it was now
her business to help her son as much as possible. Baudelaire
replied that, at her age, she must not think of such a thing.

xliii

LEAVING HIS CLOTHES and manuscripts at the hotel, he left for Paris early in July, 1865. Pincebourde made such terrifying threats that Baudelaire was obliged again to ask his mother's assistance. Madame Aupick was compelled to pay fifteen hundred francs in order to cancel the note and to get *Les Fleurs du mal* out of his control. Baudelaire returned with her to Honfleur. He tried to be cheerful, but fell into long silences in which his restlessness and anxiety were obvious to Madame Aupick. In spite of his pleasure in being back in his old room with its view of the sea, its Manets and Jongkinds and his own library, he could not be at peace. His mother, alarmed at his worn condition and his lack of appetite, made every effort to keep him with her, urging him to give up the struggle, saying that she could take care of him and manage somehow to diminish his debt.

But Baudelaire insisted upon returning to Paris to see if he could not somehow advance his interests. He took a room in the dingy Hôtel du Chemin-de-Fer-du-Nord. He visited Lemer at once. Lemer advised him that "these things move slowly"; that the business with the Garniers was still a possibility. He further urged Baudelaire to complete *Le Spleen de Paris* and to send him a detailed outline of the proposed book on Belgium, saying that the possession of these would give him an arguing point with the publishers. Moreover, without the translations of Poe, which were the property of Lévy, Lemer felt that the critical articles were too slight to make up his "complete works." On the advice of Asselineau, who thought that publishers prefer to deal directly with the author, Baudelaire went on his own account to the offices of the Garniers. He saw "the good" Garnier, that is to say Hippolyte, Auguste, "the bad one," being away on his estate in Normandy. Hippolyte could promise nothing without the concurrence of his brother, "this specimen," as Baudelaire remarked, "who enjoys himself on his estates on our money."

Baudelaire went out to Neuilly to visit Ancelle and remained in the homey bric-a-brac surroundings with the old man, whom he respected more and more, to talk about the "curious writings" of Father Hermann. He even talked with Madame Ancelle, who did not seem so flibberty-gibbet as usual.

Back in Paris, he visited Jeanne, now withered and almost completely paralyzed. He left her what money he could spare. Then he looked up his old companions. He went to see Sainte-Beuve at the offices of Le Constitutionnel, but, of course, found only the secretary, Troubat, who promised to say a word for him to the Garniers. He went to see Théodore de Banville, now a serene and respected poet, still under the proud eye of his mother, in the quietly tasteful and restful surroundings of their home. He spent a day with Asselineau still devoted and still down-at-heel and of literary inconsequence. He looked up Catulle Mendès at the offices of Le Parnasse contemporain. He met there among others Josephin Soulary and a certain haggard person by the name of Regnault who followed him around repeating "cher maître" over and over. He spent the night at the lodgings of Catulle Mendès who could not sleep for hearing the tossing and sighing of Baudelaire. In the morning, he left for Brussels and his "entirely white room which was cold even in summer."

xliv

HE RECEIVED A LETTER shortly afterward from Sainte-Beuve who apologized for not having been able to see him. Sainte-Beuve observed to Baudelaire that it had been an error for him to leave Paris; for there was now a Baudelaireian School, and there were a great many writers for whom he could act as "consulting poet." Sainte-Beuve indicated specifically a series of three articles on Baudelaire which had appeared in *Le Parnasse contemporain*, written by a bald, satyr-faced little clerk in the City Hall, by the name of Paul Verlaine. Catulle Mendès, who was the editor of *Le Parnasse contemporain*, had indeed, written to Baudelaire previously that he had accepted the paper, but had had to suggest to the writer "les grandes lignes" which the article should take, and that he would not be responsible for errors. The article stated, substantially, that, Baudelaire was the "purest poet" of the times with, of course, the exception of Victor Hugo.

It was some time before Baudelaire answered Sainte-Beuve's letter. Indeed, he was considering whether to answer it at all. Finally he wrote, thanking Sainte-Beuve for his solicitousness and observing that "it appears that there is, indeed, a Baudelaire School"; but, although many of these young writers have talent, "what a lack of substance, what lack of precision, what faulty language!" Baudelaire also took the opportunity to inform Sainte-Beuve that he had just re-read his *Consolations* and was now convinced that, "as a child," he did not lack taste. Baudelaire further congratulated Sainte-Beuve on the fine portrait of him as a Senator of the Empire, which appeared in *L'Illustration*. "You are now," Baudelaire continued, "the equal of many mediocre people; and, if you are happy, I am content."

He set to work making a detailed outline of "Pauvre Belgique!" for Lemer. When finished, it covered some fifty pages of closely written manuscript. He sent it off, asking Lemer to take care of it and assuring him that he was now hurrying to complete *Le Spleen de Paris*. But Lemer's tergiversations continued. Baudelaire became so upset at Lemer's evasiveness and delays that, touched by Ancelle's honest devotion, he wrote to him, "Make yourself a literary agent for me and see if you cannot do better than this fellow Lemer."

After Baudelaire's translation of the *Satyricon*, for his study of Choderlos de Laclos was not progressing, Poulet-Malassis conceived the idea of bringing out the poems from *Les Fleurs du mal* which had been condemned by the French courts, together with some of the Belgian violences of Baudelaire, and have the book preceded by a frontispiece by Félicien Rops done in that sub-pornographic but honestly artistic manner of which Rops was master. Poulet-Malassis felt that the publication of this might help the two of them to recapture their fortunes fairly quickly. Baudelaire sent with the sheaf of condemned and later poems, prose sketches which were les dessous of the cycle on Jeanne and which were released more out of desperation than choice. They were like sketches in the nude of a fine female torso with added observations a young and flippant artist might make in anger or disgust at his model.

But, at that time, Catulle Mendès published a group of Baudelaire's poems in *Le Parnasse contemporain*. Some of these were reprinted from other publications, for the most part no longer in existence. None had appeared in either of the first two editions of *Les Fleurs du mal*; and Baudelaire had planned to use them in a third. This group contained, among others, "L'Épigraphe pour un livre condamné," "L'Examen de minuit," "Le Couvercle," "Le Jet d'eau," "La Voix," "Le Gouffre," "Les Plaintes d'un Icare" and "Recueillement." "L'Épigraphe pour un livre condamné" warned "the peaceful, bucolic reader; the sober, naïve citizen" not to read *Les Fleurs du mal,* that "sad, saturnian and orgiastic book." They would think him "hysterical." But if you are "curious and have suffered, seeking a paradise,"

> Ame curieuse qui souffres
> Et vas cherchant ton paradis,[1]

if you can learn to love and have pity, read; "if not, be damned." "Le Jet d'eau" is a kind of farewell gesture to the dying beauty of Jeanne, a memory of her "with closed eyes, in the careless pose in which love surprised" her; and, when her soul, like the fountain, has lifted toward the heavens and has fallen back in languor:

> . . . mourante,
> En un flot de triste langueur [2]

"La Voix" is an effort to understand his duality. When he was young, two voices spoke to him. One said, "the earth is an endless cake" of pleasure; the other, "come beyond the possible, beyond the known":

> Au delà du possible, au delà du connu.

From then began his anguish. He became the victim of "ecstatic clairvoyance"; from then on, "like a prophet," he began to love the desert and the sea, and so often fell be-

[1] Curious soul that suffers
And goes seeking a paradise.
"Épigraphe pour un livre condamné."
[2] . . . dying
In a flood of sad languor.
"Le Jet d'eau."

cause his eyes were upon the sky. But "a voice consoled him," saying, "keep your dreams."

The remaining poems, whatever the date of their first appearance, described and emphasized the condition of his mind and soul in 1865 and 1866. "Le Couvercle," which was the only distinctly new poem in the group, described the sky as a lid upon the pot of humanity, a wall "lighted like an opera bouffe,"

> . . . le Ciel! ce mur de caveau qui l'éouffe [1]

which one regards with terror. "Le Gouffre," repeats the same sentiment with the figure of Pascal's abyss, which went with him always and which is the negation of all action, word or dream. The poem is a repetition of his terror of annihilation, with always above "the emptiness, the terrifying silence,"

> . . . vague horreur, menant on ne sait où.[2]

"And God," he adds, "with a learned hand, has drawn, against the background of my nights, an endless nightmare,"

> . . . Un cauchemar multiforme et sans trêve.[3]

From every window, he saw nothing but Infinity; and he feared sleep like the grave. In "Les Plaintes d'un Icare," he complains that, while men lie happy with their prostitutes, his arms are "weary with embracing mists"; his eyes see only now "remembered suns":

[1] . . . the sky, that wall of the cave which stifles.
          "Le Couvercle."
[2] . . . vague horror leading one knows not where.
          "Le Gouffre."
[3] . . . a nightmare many formed and endless.
          "Le Gouffre."

. . . mes yeux consumés ne voient
Que des souvenirs de soleils.[1]

In vain, he has sought the limits of space; and, "under eye
of fire," his wings break. And, "burned by the love of the
beautiful, I shall not even have the honor of giving my name
to the abyss which will be my grave." Yet in this tremendous
struggle of his spirit, in this last effort of the flesh to domi-
nate, he became suddenly capable of a magnificent resignation.

"Recueillement," the most beautiful of all these later
poems, is the restatement of the sentiments of a poem with
the same title written at the Collège Royal in Lyon when he
was fourteen years old. He had passed a slip of paper with
the poem, during the lesson, to a schoolfellow named Hignard. Hignard, who became Dean of the Faculty of Letters
at the University of Dijon, kept the poem all his life; and,
later, made it public as Baudelaire's reputation grew after
his death, to compare it with the later poem. The boyhood
poem is an astounding perfection. The feeling, the thought,
the music are as profound as the treatment is mature. It
states, with clarity and without any childish weakness of
sentiment, the tragedy of the human with a clear sense of the
ideal: "Who has not groaned and said to God, 'Pardon,
Lord, if no one loves me, if no one has my heart. They have
all corrupted me.' " Then, weary of the world and vain
speech, one lifts one's eyes to heaven; one speaks to no one,
tells no one that he loves "only heaven," and has asked God
to cleanse him of the earth. And then, when night comes,
when "the crowd has left the pavements," "one fills like
an empty church, with silence and with peace":

[1] . . . my burned out eyes see
Only remembered suns.
                    "Les Plaintes d'un Icare."

Hélas! qui n'a gémi sur autrui, sur soi-meme,
Et qui n'a dit à Dieu: "Pardonnez-moi, Seigneur,
Si personne ne m'aime, et si nul n'a mon coeur.
Ils m'ont tous corrompu; personne ne vous aime!"

Alors, lassé du monde et de ses vains discors,
Il faut lever les yeux aux voûtes sans nuages
Et ne plus adresser qu'aux muettes images
De ceux qui n'aiment rien, consolantes amours,

Alors! Alors! il faut s'entourer de mystère,
Se fermer aux regards et sans morgue et sans fiel,
Sans dire à ses voisins: "Je n'aime que le ciel"
Dire à Dieu: "Consolez mon âme de la terre."

Tel, fermé par son prêtre, un pieux monument,
Quand, sur nos sombres toits la nuit est descendue,
Quand la foule a laissé le pavé de la rue,
Se remplit de silence et de recueillement.[1]

The later poem resumes all of Baudelaire's tragedy
smoothed over by an immense resignation. In the most majestic lines he had ever written, he speaks to his pain, asks it to
be kind, more quiet; for it had asked for night and now it

[1] Alas! Who has not pitied others, and himself,
And who has not said to God, "Forgive me, Lord,
If no one loves me, if no one has my heart.
They have all corrupted me, for lack of love for Thee.

Then weary of the world and vain speech,
One must raise one's eyes to the cloudless skies
And give only to the silent forms
Of those who love nothing, consoling love,

Then! Then! one must shut onself in secret,
Shut out the looks of others and without pretension, without bitter-
ness,
Without saying to one's neighbors: "I love only heaven"
Say to God: "Cleanse my soul of the earth."

Like a church closed by its priest
When on our sombre roofs the night has come,
When the crowd has left the pavement of the street,
One is filled with silence and with peace.
"Recueillement."

comes. While the "vile multitude, under the whip of pleasure, gathers its remorse," he asks his pain to hold him by
the hand, and see the dead years lean over the balcony of the
skies; see "smiling regret" rise from the waters and the sun
die finally under the arches of the bridges:

> Sois sage, O ma Douleur, et tiens-toi plus tranquille,
> Tu réclamais le soir, il descend; le voici:
> Une atmosphère obscure enveloppe la ville,
> Aux uns portant la paix, aux autres le souci.
>
> Pendant que des mortels la multitude vile
> Sous le fouet du Plaisir, ce bourreau sans merci,
> Va cueillir des remords dans la fête servile,
> Ma Douleur, donne-moi la main, viens par ici,
>
> Loins d'eux, vois se pencher les défuntes années
> Sur les balcons du Ciel, en robes surannées;
> Surgir du fond des eaux le Regret Souriant;
>
> Le Soleil moribond s'endormir sous une arche,
> Et comme un long linceul traînant à l'Orient,
> Entends, ma chère, entends la douce nuit qui marche.[1]

For all his hesitations and fears of the Infinite, he was as if
burned clean of the world, and he turned closer to God than
ever before.

[1] Be kind, my Pain, and be more quiet.
You asked for night; it comes and it is here,
A darkness falls about the city,
Bringing peace to some, to others care.

While the vile multitude of mortals
Under the lash of Pleasure, that merciless executioner,
Goes gathering remorse at the servile feast,
My Pain, give me thy hand, come here,

Far from them, see the dead years lean
Over the balconies of Heaven, in aged robes;
See Smiling Regret rise from the waters;

See the sun go down under the arches,
And like a long shroud moving to the East,
O hear the quiet marching of the night.
　　　　　　"Recueillement."

xlv

THE BELGIAN WINTER settled down, with its almost constant gray skies; its inevitable mud and slush. In the long, painful nights in his room, he had already read two thousand four hundred pages of the history of "these frightful people." He had even made notes of a more modern cast to add to his collection. A new Leopold had just been crowned and had marched into Brussels, preceded by a band tootling an air from Les Bouffes parisiens: "Le nouveau roi barbu s'avance." The Brussels population had made a great show of patriotism by a great deal of "public drunkenness and vomiting." "There's Belgium for you," he had written his mother.

Deschanel, one of Baudelaire's particular bêtes noires, had just given a lecture on him in Paris before a group of women, to whom he usually lectured. Ancelle had attended the lecture and had sent his own account of the proceeding, along with a clipping from Le Temps. The reporter had been amused at Deschanel's great delicacy, indeed, his reluctance, in quoting certain "suggestive or questionable" sections of Les Fleurs du mal. He had quoted only after extensive explanations and apologies; and he had been surprised that the ladies became ecstatic over these sections more than the others.

Meantime, after waiting what seemed an eternity for news from Lemer, he finally heard from Ancelle on the subject of the Garniers. Ancelle had seen a Garnier, but Auguste, "the bad one." He had given Ancelle a categorical refusal to consider republishing any of Baudelaire's works. Baudelaire was at first furious with Ancelle; but then he remembered that it was he who had asked Ancelle to act as intermediary for him. He thought that Ancelle had plunged into the business with more zeal than tact. In any case, he relented in his attitude toward Ancelle; and, in a sort of frenzy, begged him to "try Dentu, Hetzel, Lévy, Hachette, that house of pedantic school-teachers," even Didier, anybody.

Lécrivain wrote him, suggesting that he might make a more immediate sale, if he gave up all rights for a lump sum. This, Baudelaire declined absolutely to do, feeling that his name must "still have some worth in Paris"; and that his work would steadily rise in value. He was, furthermore, chagrined to see in the Belgian bookshops works of inferior criticism which were enjoying popularity and bringing their authors a considerable income.

Hugo's *Chansons des rues et des bois,* a new volume of verse from that indefatigable author's pen, had just been published and was enjoying the most prominent spot in the book-sellers' windows. The Belgian and the French newspapers were pouring floods of praise upon it; and the citizens of Brussels, for whom Hugo was the last word in poetic expression, were rapidly exhausting several editions of it. Baudelaire wrote to his mother that, while this book was an enormous financial success, to gens d'esprit it was a perfect failure. "You see," he added, "I am always praying like the Pharisee."

With the coming of the end of the year, he felt that he must try to make some suitable gifts to his mother. He walked through the mud of Brussels, seeking some small present which he might afford and, yet, which was not too mean. He found, in some out-of-the-way shop, cruets from Rouen and a few odd pieces of Delft china which he hoped would please her. "I told the packer to put screws in the cases; but he put nails. I can see what will happen when your maid, Aimée, gets at them with her hammer."

New Year 1866 was his blackest. He was more nervous than ever. He could not even keep his attention on the pictures in a picture-gallery or read more than a few lines of any book. He could not look on the face of a man or child "without feeling faint." He walked for hours in the persistent Belgian rain.

xlvi

HE KEPT TO HIS régime with intense rigorousness. Lack of money, of course, compelled him to eat even less than the doctor prescribed. He drank no tea, coffee or alcohol. Even the doctor said that he was depriving himself and that "a little wine would not hurt him." When he could afford it, he took the medicines, the valerian, Vichy and belladonna with careful regularity. But the frightful pains in the head and now through the body did not leave. If they continued, he wrote his mother, he would have to take opium which he "hated." He could "scarcely write three lines without falling." The midnight fevers recurred regularly. He used to lie awake, thinking constantly of his mother, of "the good days" when he was a child in the great room of the aged house in la Rue Saint-André-des-Arts, and in their apartment in la Rue Hautefeuille. He used to lie, "wondering wheher it was apoplexy or paralysis." He would make an effort to formulate what arrangements he must make about his work and debts in case he died. He was in terror of dying and "leaving his mother alone." He did not want her, now aged and frequently ill herself, "to be injured" by his death. Sometimes he "could not move for hours."

Madame Hugo became alarmed at his continued absence from her Wednesdays. The thought of Baudelaire's reserve discouraged her somewhat from making a personal call. She wrote saying, "Your place is at our table. Do not leave it empty. Let your cares be softened by the knowledge that we are absolutely devoted to you"; and, receiving no answer, she got in touch with Poulet-Malassis, with Rops and with Monsieur Neyt, the Belgian photographer with whom Baudelaire had become friendly. They reported his condition to her and she immediately sent her doctor. The doctor confirmed the diagnosis of Baudelaire's doctor and made a few changes in diet. Hugo invited Baudelaire to spend a week with him on "his island." Baudelaire, being too ill to go, declined. Privately, he told his friends that he could not bear to be so long with so much greatness. To his mother, he wrote, "Madame Hugo is a fine and splendid woman."

Ancelle wished to come to Brussels at once, but Baudelaire wrote his mother that she must do all in her power to prevent him; that she must be exaggerating his condition, which was simply a kind of nervous exhaustion that would soon pass; and that he would resume his work and soon return to France, which, after all, was not as stupid as other countries.

Baudelaire felt a great deal better shortly afterward. He was seen again, at Madame Hugo's and at a few cafés. He wrote to his mother that with the news he had just received from Ancelle to the effect that Dentu had also refused to publish his complete works, he was considering a new trip to Paris, and that, perhaps, Lécrivain was right, after all, in saying that most publishers prefer to deal directly with the author. He added that, however, he had several more cities to visit to complete his notes on Belgium.

xlvii

HE HAD, INDEED, arranged with Poulet-Malassis and Félicien
Rops to visit Namur. He had already been there to see the
church of Saint-Loup, and he wished to visit "this masterpiece of Jesuitical art, this sinister marvel of gallantry," the
interior of which he compared to "the inside of a catafalque,
terrible and delicious, embroidered with pink, black and
silver." He moreover would enjoy meeting again the father-
in-law of Rops who lived in Namur and was "the only man
in Belgium who spoke Latin like a Frenchman." This man
was also a maker of coffins, "masterpieces of their kind,"
Baudelaire commented, "too beautiful for the carcasses of
the Belgians." After lunch Baudelaire, Poulet-Malassis, Rops
and his father-in-law set out to visit the church together.

While admiring the curious window above the altar,
Baudelaire suddenly fell in the nave of the church. His
friends lifted him quickly, while he made a furious effort
to decline their help, saying over and over, "It is nothing."
He kept his feet the rest of the day, talking little. In the
compartment of the train returning to Brussels, he was
taken with a considerable fever, and he kept repeating,
"Close the window! Close the window!" Upon arriving in
Brussels, he insisted upon returning to his hotel alone.

A few days later, Monsieur Neyt, meeting him in the
street and finding him more strange and taciturn than ever,
invited him to dinner. At dinner time, Baudelaire had not
arrived, and Monsieur Neyt, troubled about the appearance
and manner of Baudelaire, went at once to the hotel. Baude-

laire was not there either. Monsieur Neyt then set about
systematically going through the city, looking for him at his
favorite cafés. At last, at one in the morning, Monsieur
Neyt found him in la Taverne Royale. The café was nearly
empty. There was only one drowsy waiter left. Baudelaire
was alone in a dark corner of the café with a small glass
of cognac before him, only a little of which had been drunk.
The waiter told Monsieur Neyt that the glass had been
untouched for hours. Monsieur Neyt, against violent protestations, insisted upon accompanying him home and, still
against Baudelaire's wishes, assisted him upstairs to his room
where, falling upon his bed, Baudelaire cried to Monsieur
Neyt, "Get out! Get out!"

The next morning at nine o'clock, Monsieur Neyt returned. He found Baudelaire asleep, still dressed, with his
face against the wall. The lamp was still burning. He
aroused himself on Monsieur Neyt's arrival, opened his eyes,
but he could not move and he could not speak. Neyt rushed
for a doctor who diagnosed the case as hemiplegia with con-
sequent aphasia. Half of Baudelaire's body was paralyzed.

Later in the day, he recovered partial power of speech
and was able to dictate to Monsieur Neyt a letter for Ancelle,
which read: "I cannot move. I have debts. Tell my mother
that I am ill, if you like, but do not tell her how seriously.
Excuse my blunt style. I am using someone else's pen."

Monsieur Neyt notified Poulet-Malassis and Rops at once.
Together they arranged to transfer Baudelaire to L'Institut-
Saint-Jean et Sainte-Elizabeth, a hospital in the Rue des
Cendres, directed by les soeurs hospitalières. By this time,
he could say very little, repeating violently, to the terror of
the sisters, "Sacré Saint-Ciboire! Sacré Saint-Ciboire!" sometimes not being able to complete the oath.

In a day his mother arrived in Brussels. Her first words
on entering the sick room were, "My son has suffered so

much!" He kept his eyes averted as much as possible. He became quieter for a while, and indicated as best he could that, while he could not express himself, he understood everything. She was overwhelmed by his impotent rages and by "so much feeling in his eyes."

In a week, he was able to get up and to walk with his mother in the garden. He was still, however, without the power of speech. It was decided to take him back to Paris. Accompanied by his mother and Alfred Stevens, he returned to Paris in July.

Meantime, the news which Poulet-Malassis had sent to the press, had been taken as an announcement of Baudelaire's death. Indeed, *L'Évènement* announced his death; so did *Le Temps*. *Le Temps* corrected itself the next day, adding that the news was "fortunately false." *L'Évènement* reported that, while he was not dead, he was practically so. Émile Blandet had prepared a laudatory article for the occasion of Baudelaire's death; and, upon the denial of the news, he wrote, "and my beautiful article!" Later he wrote, "There is nothing human about him but his appearance." And all during the long year of Baudelaire's illness, articles fairly teemed in the press, some sympathetic like those of Yriarte, Champfleury and Mairobet, in his old enemy *Le Figaro*. Barbey d' Aurevilly had to have his say, too, in *Le Nain jaune*. He wrote a longish article saying that, "Hugo was the father of all of us, and Théophile Gautier, the uncle." He took up the subject of those then writing under Baudelaire's influence, Xavier de Ricard, Paul Verlaine, who was "funereally funny, without the clear talent of Baudelaire"; and Stéphane Mallarmé, "with his chatter about the Azure." Sainte-Beuve had hastily written a letter of sympathy to Madame Aupick.

But there were articles like that of Feyronet in *Le Temps* who wrote that Baudelaire had gone mad; like that of Santon in *La Liberté,* who said that he was dying from the effects of opium; and like that of Jules Vallès in *La Situation,* who insisted that Baudelaire was "a ghoul, a free-thinker," and that the only valuable thing he had done was to translate Edgar Allan Poe.

Meantime, Doctor Lasègues, Baudelaire's former tutor in philosophy and now a physician, thought that it was not good for Monsieur Baudelaire to be so constantly with his mother. He was transferred to la maison de santé of a Monsieur Duval in the Rue du Dôme. Baudelaire was able to walk and, for a while, able to communicate his needs by writing on a slate; and Monsieur Duval had even prided himself on being able to teach Baudelaire to repeat after him one or two words. Here Manet and his wife visited him. Madame Sabatier came to see him. Fantin-Latour and Bracquemond called, as well as Monsieur and Madame Paul Meurice. Madame Meurice played on the small piano in the salon of the establishment some Wagner which he seemed to enjoy. Some of his Jongkinds and a Whistler were brought from Honfleur for his room.

He seemed suddenly calm. While he was still able to communicate by writing or by saying a few words, he let it be known that he wished to be alone with a priest. He asked the priest to come often. He evinced no more interest in the fate of his work. He sat for hours at his window, with his mother's great silver crucifix by him, looking steadily up into the clouds. The smile, the stare into the clouds which answered Asselineau's frequent question as to whether he could be of use to him, indicated that he was putting all his hope in God; that the world he had wanted was shattered; that he was delivered of a thing he never did believe in; and that the fragments of his Faith had come together, late but, he hoped, not too late for God. It was as if it took this terrible silence to assuage his anguish and his hunger, to turn him fully, as he was already turning, toward the God he always knew and would not have, to turn his eyes upon what he had called "that place of all the transfigurations." During the long year of his illness, this calm did not seem to leave him; and he died with the ministrations of the Church on August 31, 1867.

WORKS BY BAUDELAIRE

Les *Fleurs du mal*
Curiosités esthétiques
L'Art romantique
*Petits Poèmes en prose
(Le Spleen de Paris)*
Histoires extraordinaires
Les Paradis artificiels
Nouvelles Histoires extraordinaires
L'Aventure d'Arthur Gordon Pym
Eureka

Michel Lévy Frères
Calmann-Lévy
Paris, 1858–1882

Dernières histoires extraordinaires. Nouvelle Revue Française. Paris, 1918.

Amoenitates belgicae. J. Fort. Paris, 1925.

Années de Bruxelles. Editions de la Grenade. Paris, 1927.

Lettres autographes 1850–1865. J. Leroy. Paris, 1924.

De l'essence du rire. Kieffer. Paris, 1925.

Dernières Lettres inédites à sa mère. Editions Excelsior. Paris, 1926.

Journaux intimes—Fusées. G. Crès. Paris, 1920.

Mon cœur mis à nu. G. Crès. Paris, 1920.

Lettres inédites à sa mère. L. Conard. Paris, 1918.

Salon caricatural de 1846. Société du Mercure de France. Paris, 1932.

Oeuvres posthumes. Société du Mercure de France. Paris, 1908.

Oeuvres posthumes et lettres inédites. Maison Quantin. Paris, 1887.

Richard Wagner et Tannhäuser. E. Dentu. Paris, 1861.

Le Peintre de la vie moderne Constantin Guys. R. Kieffer. Paris, 1923.

Histoires grotesques et sérieuses. Michel Levy Frères. Paris, 1865.

Le Salut public (Numéros 1 et 2). E. Champion. Paris, 1925.

BIBLIOGRAPHY

Asselineau, Charles. *Charles Baudelaire, sa vie et son œuvre.* Lemerre. Paris, 1869.

Aubry, G. J. *Un Paysage littéraire.* Maison du Livre. Paris, 1917.

Bandy, W. T. *Baudelaire Judged by His Contemporaries.* Institute of French Studies. Columbia University, N. Y., 1933.

Barrès, Maurice. *La Folie de Charles Baudelaire.* Les Ecrivains Unis. Paris, 1926.

Berthon, Henry. *Nine French Poets.* Macmillan. New York, 1930.

Cabanès, Auguste. *Grands Nevropathes, Malades immortels.* A. Michel. Paris, 1930.

Carrière, Jean. *Degeneration in Great French Masters.* Brentano's. New York, 1922.

Caume, Pierre. *Causeries sur Baudelaire.* Nouvelle Revue Française. Paris, 1899.

Clapton, G. T. *Baudelaire, The Tragic Sophist.* Oliver & Boyd. Edinburgh, 1934.

————. *Baudelaire et DeQuincey.* Société d'Editions Les Belles Lettres. Paris, 1931.

Cousin, Charles. *Charles Baudelaire, Souvenirs.* Pincebourde. Paris, 1872.

Crépet, Eugène. *Charles Baudelaire, Etude Biographique.* L. Vanier. Paris, 1906.

Dufay, Pierre. *Autour de Baudelaire.* Au Cabinet du Livre. Paris, 1931.

Eliot, T. S. *For Lancelot Andrewes.* Faber & Gwyer. London, 1928.

Feuillerat, Albert. *Baudelaire et la belle aux cheveux d'or.* Yale University Press. New Haven, 1941.

Flotte, Pierre. *Baudelaire l'homme et poète.* Perrin & Cie. Paris, 1922.

177

Gautier, Féli. *Charles Baudelaire*. Editions de la Plume. Paris, 1903.

Gautier, Théophile. *Charles Baudelaire*. Greening & Co. London, 1915.

———. *Souvenirs romantiques*. Garnier Frères. Paris, 1929.

Huneker, Charles. *Egoists*. Scribners. New York, 1909.

Kahn, Gustave. *Charles Baudelaire et son Oeuvre*. Editions La Nouvelle Revue Critique. Paris, 1925.

Laforgue, René. *L'Echec de Baudelaire*. Denoël et Steele. Paris, 1931.

Lavrin, Yanko. *Studies in European Literature*. Constable & Co. London, 1929.

Lemonnier, Leon. *Enquêtes sur Baudelaire*. Crès. Paris, 1929.

L'Isle-Adam, V. de. *Lettres à Charles Baudelaire*. Nouvelle Revue Française. Paris, 1903.

Porché, François. *Charles Baudelaire*. Wishart & Co. London, 1928.

———. *La Vie douloureuse de Charles Baudelaire*. Plon. Paris, 1926.

Quennell, Peter. *Baudelaire and the Symbolists*. Chatto & Windus. London, 1929.

Raymond, Marcel. *De Baudelaire au surréalisme*. Corréa. Paris, 1933.

Raymond, Ernest. *Charles Baudelaire*. Garnier Frères. Paris, 1922.

Reynold, Gonzague de. *Charles Baudelaire*. Crès. Paris, 1920.

Rhodes, S. A. *The Cult of Beauty in Charles Baudelaire*. Columbia University Press. New York, 1929.

Rivière, Jacques. *Etudes*. Gallimard. Paris, 1924.

Séché, Alphonse. *Charles Baudelaire*. Michaude. Paris, 1910.

Shanks, Lewis P. *Baudelaire, Flesh & Spirit*. Little, Brown. Boston, 1930.

Souppault, Philippe. *Baudelaire*. Rieder. Paris, 1931.

Starkie, Enid. *Baudelaire*. Putnam. New York, 1933.

Suarès, André. *Trois Grands Vivants*. Grasset. Paris, 1937.

Swinburne, Algernon. *A Pilgrimage of Pleasure*. Badger. Boston, 1913.

Symons, Arthur. *Charles Baudelaire*. Mathews. London, 1920.

Turquet-Milnes, G. *The Influence of Baudelaire*. Constable. London, 1913.

Valéry, Paul. *Variety*. Harcourt, Brace. New York, 1938.

Vivier, Robert. *L'Originalité de Baudelaire*. Académie Royale. Bruxelles, 1926.

————. *La Fiche Bibliographique Française*. Bibliothèque Nationale de Paris.

And files of British, French and American newspapers and periodicals